Awaken to the Buddha Within

Shi Wuling

Venerable Wuling is an American Buddhist nun of the Pure Land
school of Mahayana Buddhism.

Amitabha Publications, Chicago, 60532
© 2006 by Amitabha Publications
Published 2006
No part of this book may not be altered without permission from the
publisher. Reprinting is allowed for non-profit use.
For the latest edition, contact www.amitabha-publications.org
Printed in Taiwan

11 10 09 08 07 06   1 2 3 4 5 6

ISBN: 978-1-59975-355-3

Ottawa Amitabha Buddhist Society of Canada
7 Campfield Court, Ottawa, ON K2E 7X9
Tel: (613) 723-9683   Fax: (613) 723-6316
www.amtb-ottawa.ca

CONTENTS

ACKNOWLEDGEMENTS

With deep appreciation, I thank all those who have contributed to this book: family, friends, fellow students, and teachers. Without their support and patience, this book could never have come into being.

I thank my teacher, Master Chin Kung, who over the past decade has wisely taught me the principles that are woven throughout this book. I thank my fellow students and friends who have so kindly taken the time to serve as consultants and editors. I also thank those who generously provided the funds for printing. Any errors that remain are my own.

I am deeply grateful to my parents, Milton and Evelyn Bolender, who provided the opportunity for me to follow my path in this lifetime. Without them, this book, my life, would never have happened. My gratitude to them can never be repaid.

Shi Wuling

BUDDHISM TODAY

One day, a famous government official, who was also a poet, was passing along a road. He saw an old monk teaching Buddhism. This was hardly unusual except that the monk was seated on a tree branch. The official asked the elderly monk what he was doing. After all, the monk was in a very precarious position. One wrong move and he could fall to his death!

The monk replied that the official's position was even more precarious. If the monk made a careless move, he alone might be killed. But if the official made a mistake, it could cost the lives of thousands.

The official considered this and decided that it was a very good reply. He told the monk that if he could explain the essence of Buddhism in one sentence, then he would become the monk's student. "Easy!" said the monk. "The essence of Buddhism is to avoid all that is evil, to embrace all that is good, and to purify one's mind." The official scoffed, "Is that all? Even a child of three knows that!" The monk replied that while it was true that a child of three may realize it, there was no certainty that a man of eighty could practice it.

The master in our story was absolutely right. It is one thing to know what we are supposed to do; doing so is an entirely different matter. But without doing what is good, we will be unable to benefit others or ourselves: We will be unable to help all beings find their way to genuine happiness and secure their liberation from suffering.

How do we begin to realize the truth? And then how do we think and behave when we have done so? We can begin by looking at how Buddhism is viewed and defined today. Many people respect Buddhism for its strong ethical belief system, which focuses on training one's own mind and body rather than on controlling others. Buddhism is valued for its teachings, which stress the daily observance of compassion for all beings, and for its emphasis on understanding the eternal principles of life, which will lead us to awaken our innate wisdom.

Anyone can practice the various meditation methods, as well as the chanting of mantras or of a Buddha's name. All of these will help to increase one's awareness and concentration, which can help lead one to awakening, or simply enable one to attain a calmer and clearer mind.

Buddhism has a long history of the practice of equanimity and peace. A war has never been declared in its name. And in a world which has seen untold suffering from war, a belief system that focuses on looking within to overcome one's own shortcomings, not on conquering other people, is highly respected.

Understanding and practicing the teachings will enable us to find the answers to our questions and to learn how to lead more meaningful lives. Like all good teachings, what the Buddha taught can benefit all people, Buddhists and non-Buddhists alike.

Today, many people regard Buddhism as a religion. *Merriam-Webster's Collegiate Dictionary* defines religion as "the service and worship of God." But Buddhas are not gods. The person whom we know as the Buddha, over many lifetimes, uncovered the goodness, compassion, and wisdom that lay within his true nature. He achieved supreme enlightenment and in doing so became an example of what we, too, can achieve: We have within each of us our true nature, our own Buddha-nature, that is waiting to be fully awakened.

Once, the Buddha was asked if he was a god. The Buddha replied that, no, he was not a god. Then was he an angel? No. A spirit? No. Then what was he? The Buddha replied that he was awakened. Since the Buddha, by his own explanation, is not a god, we do not worship him. We respect and are grateful to him for teaching us the Way to be liberated from the cycle of birth, death, and rebirth, and to become perfectly enlightened just as he was.

Religion is also considered a belief in a supernatural power or powers regarded as the creator and ruler of the universe. But the Buddha is neither.

The Buddha did not create the universe. Having observed the reality of basic eternal principles, he explained that everything arises from our minds. In effect, the universe is the creation of all our thoughts and behavior, not the creation of any one being.

Neither does the Buddha govern the universe. The natural law of causality determines what will happen. Simply put, we reap what we sow. If we plant the seeds for wheat, we will harvest wheat. Likewise, if we plant the seeds for kindness, for example, by caring for others, we will receive kindness in turn. We have already sown the seeds, some good and some bad. Some lie dormant within us, just as others have already matured.

We bear the consequences of our thoughts, speech, and actions that we initiated in the past. No other being, no matter how wise or compassionate, can bear the consequences on our behalf. We alone are responsible for our individual lives. Just as our lives today are the direct results of what we did in the past, what we do today will, similarly and unequivocally, create our future.

It is the belief of many religions that heaven and hell are permanent and everlasting. As Buddhists, we believe that while our lives in the heaven and hell realms are eons long and may therefore seem eternal, they are not. We rise and fall through the realms of existence as our good actions help us to rise to better lifetimes while our bad behavior literally brings us down. We rise again, only to fall yet again. We have done this, over and over again, innumerable times. Some lifetimes last just a matter of days. Others last longer than we can possibly imagine. But within the realms of existence, of which heaven and hell are a part, no life is permanent. And no lifetime is eternal. Because of this aimless recycling, Buddhists seek to transcend this cycle through awakening, through enlightenment.

What about the concept of Buddhism as a philosophy? By studying Buddhism in this context, people will likely fail to achieve lasting benefits because they will not practice the teachings. And without practice, no one can achieve enlightenment. Also, philosophy is just one field studied in school, whereas Buddhism actually encompasses and transcends every single field. In regards to time, Buddhism encompasses the past, present, and future. In regards to space, it encompasses everything: from our daily lives to the infinite universe.

So if Buddhism is neither a religion nor a philosophy, what is it? Buddhism is a way of understanding life and the universe, and of practicing that understanding to end unhappiness. It is a way of life and a state of mind. Buddhism is a teaching: a systematic learning of eternal truths.

In the sutras, which are recorded teachings of the Buddha, and occasionally of bodhisattvas, we read that he was spoken of as our original teacher. Those who listened to him were called students. When the students asked questions of the Buddha, he would often reply with another question. This was to help the students realize the answer for themselves. If the students did not thoroughly understand, or if they thought that the Buddha's future students would not thoroughly understand, they would seek further clarification by asking more questions. These sesssions were essentially classroom discussions that followed the pattern we call the Socratic method, a method exemplified by the Greek philosopher Socrates, who lived in Greece well after the Buddha lived in India.

The Buddha did not conduct ceremonies. He simply taught and practiced what he taught. As a teacher, he stepped out of the confines of the time in which he lived through his concept of equality. Instead of adhering to the caste system, he treated untouchables with equality and respect. He accepted women as nuns, at a time when women were regarded as another form of property. He was against animal sacrifice and appealed to people to respect and not harm any living creature. These were very progressive views from someone who lived almost three millennium ago.

HE WHO HAS
ACCOMPLISHED HIS GOAL

Who was the Buddha and how had such a being come to exist? Over twenty-six hundred years ago, a clan named Sakya ruled one of the many small kingdoms in an area that is now in the foothills of Nepal. The king's given name was Suddhodana and his family name was Gautama. One night, his wife Queen Maya had a dream which she related to her husband. When dream interpreters were brought to the palace, they said the dream foretold the queen bearing a son who would either be a great king or a universal teacher.

After the prince was born, he was named Siddhartha, which means "he who has accomplished his goal." A revered ascetic, Master Asita, came to the palace to see the child. First, a smile brightened his face when he saw the new prince. But then, a tear fell from his eye and rolled slowly down his face. He began to weep, with more tears streaming down. Greatly concerned, the king asked if some terrible misfortune was to befall his son. Master Asita replied no. On the contrary, the child would grow up to one day find the Way to enlightenment. But he, Asita, would no longer be alive, and so he wept.

Just a few days after Siddhartha's birth, the queen died and the prince was raised by his aunt, the king's second wife. She lovingly cared for Siddhartha as if he were her own son.

When Siddhartha was nine years old he went to the annual plowing ceremony. He saw the panting oxen being lashed by their sweating handlers while the sun blazed overhead. And as the plows tore into the earth, he saw the worms being cut up by the plowing. Small birds swooped down to devour the writhing creatures. A larger bird flew down and caught a smaller one. Siddhartha contemplated what he had just seen. Even as a child, he was becoming aware of the harsh realities of life—all living beings kill one another to survive and in this there is suffering.

As Siddhartha grew up, he was provided with everything a young prince could have: the finest possessions, the most learned teachers, and a beautiful palace in which to live. But, instead of becoming spoiled, his humble demeanor inspired trust in others. Through it all, he remained respectful and gentle towards all. And as time passed, his concern for the welfare of others took root and began to grow stronger.

In an effort to bring his pensive son's thoughts back to a more worldly existence as well as to his princely responsibilities as the future ruler, the king decided that Siddhartha needed to get married.

Various gatherings of young people were arranged and one young woman in particular, Siddhartha's cousin, the princess Yasodhara, stood out from the others. She was not only beautiful in appearance, but had inner strength as well. Like Siddhartha, she was thoughtful and cared deeply for those who suffered from poverty and illness.

The prince and princess were married. They lived in three palaces: They enjoyed the summer in a palace made of cool marble. In the winter, they stayed warm in a palace made of fragrant wood. The monsoon season was passed comfortably in a brick palace with a high green tile roof.

Siddhartha and Yasodhara were provided with

everything they could have wanted. They were privileged with the finest possessions. Musicians and dancers were housed in the palaces to entertain the royal couple.

Then came the events that are known as the Four Sights. This account tells of how the sheltered prince is said to have encountered, for the first time, the reality of the universal hardships of old age, sickness, and death, in spite of his father's attempts to shield him from them. He also saw a monk, a religious seeker of truth, who radiated peace and serenity.

Siddhartha learned that not only animals suffer, but that all of humanity is subject to aging, sickness, death, and separation from loved ones. Siddhartha felt the pain and loss undergone by all beings. But he could do nothing to save his people from the inevitable pain that lay in their future. More and more, this gentle and contemplative young man found himself being drawn into this universal problem. He wanted with all his heart to find the way to end the pain for all beings.

Siddhartha was deeply troubled. Although he was a skilled warrior, he knew he could not solve humanity's problems by warfare. Although he was the future king, he knew he could not help end the distress of others through political decisions alone. The learned prince became increasingly aware that he could not resolve suffering through worldly knowledge.

More than ever Siddhartha felt questions arise within him: How does one find lasting peace? How does one move beyond the reach of illness and death? How does one find the Way for all beings? It was the fourth encounter—the memory of that serene monk—that gave Siddhartha hope that there was an answer out there, somewhere.

One morning, Siddhartha went to his father and requested permission to leave home to become a monk. King Suddhodana must have known that this day might come, but so soon? Could Siddhartha not wait? His father sincerely respected the tradition of renouncing one's worldly life to seek a more spiritual one. But this was usually done when one was older, not when one has a young family and so many responsibilities as the future king! Siddhartha persisted for his father could not end Siddhartha's suffering any more than Siddhartha could end his father's. Siddhartha assured his father that he would return when he had found the Way.

That night Siddhartha went to his quarters. He gazed intensely at his sleeping newborn son. Yasodhara also seemed to be asleep. He quietly left the room. He loved them intensely so he had to do whatever he could to find the Way to free them from pain and distress. Knowing that they would be lovingly taken care of, Siddhartha quietly slipped out of the palace to find the way to end suffering for them, for those he was responsible for, and for all beings.

Siddhartha was a man with everything: youth, wealth, and position. He was admired for his cleverness and bravery as well as his wisdom. He had proven himself to be the greatest warrior in the matches that were held in the kingdom, but he was also known for his kind heart. Siddhartha had a beautiful wife who loved him and whom he loved. She had given birth to their son. But, he realized that with all that he possessed and with all that he knew, he could not protect them from aging, sickness, and death.

Siddhartha renounced his existence as a prince who by his royal birth, unmatched capabilities, and great strength of character would have been a great king, and instead, became Gautama, a wandering seeker of the Way. He gave up material security and future power to live under the trees, and to forage and beg for his food. He rejected fine clothes and jewels to wear cast-off rags. He relinquished fleeting worldly love to search for the Way to permanent love and liberation, which no man had found.

When Gautama learned that Master Alara Kalama, a highly respected teacher was nearby, he made his way to the master's center. Gautama was accepted as a student and quickly mastered the practice he was given. He went back to the master who then taught him how to attain the next meditative state. But even the attainment of this state did not provide the answers to Gautama's questions of how to end the cycle of birth, death, and rebirth, and how to liberate humanity from pain and distress. Gautama gratefully thanked the master for his teachings and declined an invitation to teach alongside him. He respectfully took his leave and continued to practice and search for the answers.

After a while, he learned that another teacher, Master Udakka Ramaputta, was close by. Gautama went to him and requested to become a student. This time as well, he quickly learned from his teacher. He transcended all ordinary planes of consciousness and remained in a state of great tranquility. But when he came out of meditation, the problems of life and death were still there. He thanked the master for his teachings and politely declined the offer to remain and become the new master upon Master Udakka Ramaputta's death.

At this point, Gautama had practiced under the guidance of two of the most respected teachers of meditation. He had mastered everything they could teach. But, he still had not learned how to permanently end suffering. He realized that he had reached the point where he must discover the Way himself.

After a period of solitary practice, he was joined by five ascetics who became his companions. Over the ensuing months they lived in a group of caves and in nearby forests. As Gautama intensified his practice he ate only a handful of food a day. Then, Gautama reduced his food intake to less than a mouthful a day.

He sat in meditation and ignored the blazing heat and freezing cold. His body became emaciated. His bones were as brittle as dry sticks, his ribs were like exposed rafters, and his vertebrae were like beads on a string. His eyes sank deep into his skull. His hair fell out at his touch. When he touched the skin on his stomach, he could feel his backbone. The five ascetics who were with him could not match his rigorous practice.

Then, one day, while meditating in a cemetery, Gautama suddenly realized that the traditional religious teachings, his attainment of elevated states of meditation, and his practice of extreme austerities had all failed to disclose the solution to end pain and distress for the benefit of all beings! If he died from all his exertions, what would he have accomplished for others?

He thought of the peace that he had known in earlier meditations. Mind and body both needed to be healthy to be able to find the way to enlightenment. One's mind needed to be peaceful and focused. One's body needed to be strong and healthy.

The next morning, Gautama went to the river to bathe. When he finished he managed to drag himself up the riverbank, but he had only gone a little way when he collapsed from sheer weakness. He might have died had it not been for a passing village girl, on her way to make offerings to the forest gods, who gave him some rice-milk. As he drank more of the milk, some of his strength gradually returned, and he began to see the unity among all things. Mind and body are interconnected. The wisdom of the universe was to be found in each and every cell. Self-inflicted deprivation was not the answer. There was already enough pain in the world.

Gautama decided to give up his austere practices and to live in the forest near the river. He had realized "the Middle Way," which bridges ascetic denial and sensual attachment in a balanced middle ground. His companions saw him eating more food, talking with the girl who sometimes brought it to him, and no longer following the traditional ways of austere practice. They believed that he had abandoned his seeking of the Way and returned to worldly pleasures. So the five left him, deeply disappointed at his seeming weakness and lack of resolve.

Gautama continued to meditate alone. He realized that everything which came into existence, living and non-living, was interconnected to everything else. Nothing existed on its own. He also understood that nothing was permanent and that everything was changing continuously.

THE GREAT AWAKENING

Gautama's thoughts kept returning to his questions: How does one end unhappiness and pain? How does one protect loved ones from sickness and death? Indulging oneself in sensual pleasures was certainly not the solution.

The traditional beliefs had likewise failed to provide the way to end suffering. Many priests distanced themselves from the pain around them. They sacrificed animals while ignoring the cries of pain and terror as the animals desperately struggled to live. All life, human and animal, was to be protected and cherished. Thus, the traditional beliefs were not the answer either.

Gautama also understood that his sitting in meditation as instructed by the two masters had not enabled him to elevate himself above worldly pain. As soon as he left his contemplative state, he returned to a world of birth, aging, sickness, and death. He had not yet found the way to end them.

Extreme disciplines and intense deprivation were also not the answers. It was thought that if one practiced severe austerities, one could achieve rebirth in heaven. But even a lifetime in heaven would end one day because the heavenly realms are still within the cycle of rebirth. And besides, the unhappiness and pain of those who remained on earth would still continue unabated.

Torturing one's body results in the mind being afflicted as well, not in its finding peace. So while the body is not to be indulged, it should not be abused either. It is much wiser to properly care for one's body so that it is able to carry one along the path to enlightenment.

Gautama's ascetic practice, which sought to remove desire, had resolved nothing. Mind and body are not separate. They are intrinsically linked to each other. No, abusing one's body would not help one to find the answer either. After six years, Gautama realized, just at the point of death, that what he had achieved in his practice would only benefit himself, temporarily. All around him, humanity was still suffering.

Gautama would have to find the Way himself. It seemed to lie in a more balanced approach to meditation. He would later use the example of a lute: If the strings of the lute were too tight, the sound would be unpleasant and the strings would most likely break. If they were too loose, the sound would not be harmonious. The strings needed to be properly tuned to produce a pleasing sound. Just as the beauty of a lute can only reveal itself when the strings are properly tuned, the attainment of serenity can only be found when one's life is well balanced.

One needed serenity as well as compassion and wisdom to end humanity's pain and unhappiness. Understanding what he needed to do, the once future king sat down on a pile of grass beneath the tree he had often sat under and slowly assumed a meditation position. He vowed that even if only his skin, sinews, and bones remained, and his blood dried up and flesh withered away, he would not stir from his seat until he had attained supreme, perfect enlightenment.

He heard the gentle sounds of birds and insects and the murmur of the river. He felt a soft breeze against his skin. The air smelled fresh. He lightly closed his eyes. Slowly the breeze died and the sounds around him became mere whispers.

Perfectly calm on the outside, alert and determined within, he was ready. As he moved with ease deeper into his meditation, Mara came. Mara is all that is negative within us and arises when we wish to awaken from our seemingly endless sleep. Mara brought forth many demons including those of egotism, doubt, passion, pride, and ignorance to destroy Gautama's resolve and attainment. Gautama subdued them all.

He moved deeper still into meditation, into a state unfathomable to ordinary beings. As if he was on a high mountain looking down at every river he had ever crossed and every rock he had scaled on the way to reaching the summit, he clearly saw all his past lives. They were joined by a seemingly unbreakable karmic chain that bound him to countless births and rebirths, without reward or respite.

He moved deeper still into his meditative state and saw formation and cessation. He looked beyond this world to other galaxies throughout the universe and saw worlds take form, exist, and then end. He saw innumerable beings passing through countless lifetimes, still lost, still wandering. He saw the eternal law of cause and effect that governed all worlds, including ours, working in all aspects of our lives: He understood how current actions, speech, thoughts—everything—determined the future. Good produces good. Evil incurs evil. Causes mature into results that, in turn, become new causes.

Thunder cracked, lightning tore the sky, and rain poured down, soaking Gautama, who remained motionless throughout. He continued his inward quest. He saw that the poisons of greed, anger, arrogance, and doubt are all rooted in our ignorance. With giving, we can let go of greed. With patience, we can dissolve anger. With wisdom, we can sweep away ignorance, arrogance, and doubt.

People behave as they do because of past thoughts, words, and actions, but they do not know this. One person will act out of ignorance while another will react from the same ignorance, and so they become more tightly bound to each other. All humanity—all beings—are bound by that slim, invisible chain that strangles all who do not see. This chain is ignorance. And only the sword of wisdom, which arises when one is selfless, can sever it. When one lets go of ego, one sees that we are all one, that we are all interrelated.

Gautama transcended the ordinary levels of consciousness. Finally, he found the answers he had been seeking. They would become the core of his teachings—the Four Noble Truths. Life is suffering. Suffering is caused. Suffering can end. The way to its end lies along the path of discipline, concentration, and wisdom.

The black clouds cleared. The thunder and lightning ceased. As he looked up and gazed at the sky, he knew he had found the Way to supreme enlightenment. Ignorance leads to craving, craving to rebirth, rebirth to suffering. Suffering has a cause and an end.

No longer would he have to be reborn. For him, the chain no longer existed. He had severed it with the sword of wisdom. He was fully liberated. This was his last birth.

He smiled as he gazed upon the new dawn. There was no more pain, no more sorrow, only infinite peace and a profound, unconditional love for all beings. Now, after his innumerable lifetimes wandering through the valley, his growing discontent as the prince named Siddhartha, his six years of striving as the wandering seeker Gautama, and his night of awakening, he had finally reached the summit and found the Way to teach all beings how to end their pain and unhappiness. He was now "Buddha," fully awakened.

Gautama remained in the forest for forty-nine days and thought of how to teach others what he had just experienced. He had finally perceived everything and in doing so eliminated the ignorance that bound him. But the rest of humanity was still trapped in ignorance. Being able to see only a minute portion of reality, they were easily misled by misperceptions and personal views. They could not yet truly see.

They did not yet realize that everyone has within themselves the same nature that he, the Buddha, has. Today, we still do not truly see. Indeed, every living being has this true nature. Thus, all beings are, by nature, equal. By nature, no human is superior to any animal or any living being. Like Gautama, humanity has the ability to discover the undistorted truth of the universe. If people can discover this truth, they too can liberate themselves.

And so it was time to teach what he had learned. He used different methods to teach different people.

To teach those who were learned, he used logic and his understanding of the religious teachings. For those who were intuitive, he used images and actions, not speech. For those who were simple, he spoke only a few necessary words. And for those who were suffering, he showed that all beings underwent pain and unhappiness.

It was time to leave the peace of the forest. First, he looked for Master Alara Kalama and Master Udakka Ramaputta, and then, his five former companions, for he knew they were ready to understand what he could teach them. Wearing the robe provided by the girl who had given him the rice-milk, he set out.

On the way, the Buddha met a monk who had been a student of the two masters he was seeking. He learned from the monk that both of his former teachers had died. Regretfully, it was too late to share what he had learned with the two accomplished masters who so generously taught him everything they knew. He then enquired about the five ascetics and learned where they were practicing. The Buddha headed north to find them.

After many days of walking he reached Deer Park,

where the five were staying. When they saw him approaching they discussed what to do. They remembered how he had stopped his austere practice, begun to eat more, and interacted with the local people. They had rejected and left him. Now here he was again! They decided that they would pay no attention to him and not even stand to properly greet him.

But as the Buddha approached, they were unable to ignore him. His appearance was radiant, his bearing dignified yet gentle. The five ascetics had achieved much understanding. Perhaps they realized that this was no longer an ordinary man. They quickly took his begging bowl and gave him a stool to sit on and some fresh water to drink. Only then did they sit down on the ground around him.

The Buddha told them that he had found what they were seeking. At first, no one spoke. Then they questioned how could one who had abandoned his ascetic ways and begun eating more food have possibly found the Way?

The Buddha asked if they had ever heard him lie or previously claim that he had achieved the Way. They replied that they had not. Then would the five listen to him so he could tell them what he had learned? They requested the Buddha to teach them.

The Buddha told them that what he had learned was not the result of any analytical thinking, but of having seen reality. Those who seek the Way should neither immerse themselves in sensual pleasures nor deprive their bodies of essential needs, but follow the path of moderation. He explained that all beings who live in this world are subject to four basic truths. The first three are that suffering exists, it is caused, and it has an end.

The fourth truth explains how to end suffering through the proper practice of discipline, concentration, and wisdom. This course of conduct neither denies nor avoids suffering. It faces suffering and transforms it. The practice of discipline, concentration, and wisdom will ultimately lead one to liberation, peace, and joy.

Turning the Dharma Wheel: The Four Noble Truths

In life, there is suffering. Suffering is caused. Suffering can end. The way to its end is through the practice of discipline, concentration, and wisdom.

It might seem pessimistic for the Buddha to say that in life there is much unhappiness. But he did not leave it at that, for like a good doctor, he diagnosed the fundamental problem of life and declared it: Life involves suffering. Like a good doctor, he wanted to help all beings so that they would attain the understanding that would lead to awakening and, thus, obtain permanent release from this distress. He was not concerned with worldly or spiritual speculation but with how to help all beings achieve liberation.

And like a caring doctor, he optimistically determined that a cure exists, and prescribed the requisite treatment as embodied in the Four Noble Truths:

right understanding and proper practice. The Four Noble Truths provide the solution to our unhappiness. We need to understand and abandon suffering and its cause, and embrace the proper way of living. This statement is surely one of optimism, not pessimism.

Upon hearing that in life there is much suffering, people often say that they do not "suffer." We might understand better the meaning of suffering if we think of it as describing life as never being completely satisfactory. We very often feel some degree of physical or mental discomfort. At other times in our lives, we all undergo genuine pain. Initially, we experience the trauma of birth; later, we encounter disease and illness. Many of us will go through aging, and none of us will escape death. We are all subject to the emotional hardships of pain and grief as we undergo the mental distress of failing to attain what we wish. All too often, we find ourselves having to tolerate the presence of those we dislike or, perhaps, even hate. And eventually we will be separated from all those we love. These are all forms of suffering. As Siddhartha had learned, even a king is helpless in the face of aging and death.

Regardless of whether we say life entails pain or it

is never completely satisfactory, all beings are subject to distress. Simply put, things usually do not go as we wish. For example, we may find ourselves having to move away from those we love. Often at work, we need to interact with or report to people who do not think the same way we do, and, thus, our workplace becomes a place of antagonism and stress. Or we may have to watch helplessly as those we love must endure an illness for which there is no cure.

Our suffering is the disappointment, bitterness, and helplessness we feel. When things do not go as we wish, life is very often unfulfilling, and even if it is not painful, it is certainly unsatisfactory. When we do get what we wish, we find that good things and good times do not last.

For example, for those who have not been able to eat their favorite food for a long time, the sudden appearance of it can bring great happiness. Upon seeing the food and detecting its aroma, we will smile in anticipation. The consumption of it brings pleasure as we savor the taste. Memories of the past enjoyment of it come flooding back. Remembering the people we used to share it with brings a feeling of contentment.

But what if we overeat? Within our enjoyment lies the seed of distress as we give in to our senses and eat too much. No longer happy, we now feel uncomfortable and may even become ill. Happiness turns into displeasure because happiness contains within it future discontent. And even if we do not overeat, even reasonable eating only temporarily stops our discomfort. Very soon we are hungry again and distressed again. And the loss of our recent happiness becomes another source of distress.

Pleasure from any worldly activity inevitably turns into distress whenever it goes beyond the bounds of moderation, whether it is walking, reading, eating that favorite food, or any other interest that we enjoy. When we begin walking, initially it is very enjoyable, but after a certain amount of time it can become exhausting and painful. After many hours of reading our favorite author's latest book, our eyes become tired. We feel stiff from lack of movement, and we feel the need to move around. Thus, pleasure can in itself become discontent. But a painful experience does not naturally become pleasant. To counteract the pain, one needs to change what one is doing.

Suffering is inherent in everything within our exis-

tence. Thus, this is the first truth: In life there is suffering. What is its cause? Ignorance and greed. Ignorance is the lack of understanding that all condi-
tioned things are impermanent and are void of an
everlasting individual identity. Greed is the craving
and attachment for material things or pleasant experiences or anything else. We probably think that
we are not greedy; it is others who have greed: We
only have reasonable wishes.

If you feel that all your needs are reasonable,
please reconsider. Think of one of your most treasured possessions. Picture it in your mind. Now, think
of giving it away. What do you feel? If you are like
most of us, you will find that it is very discomforting
to consider giving away a treasured possession. This
is attachment. Attachments are our emotional desires for people, pleasures, ideas, and so on. Our attachments and, therefore, our cravings lead us to
think that controlling others or having things will
make us happy.

But so very often, every time we acquire something, its appeal soon fades. We then would like a
newer version or a different color or a fancier style.
This is greed.

It is like taking a child to a toy store. The child does everything possible to get his parents to purchase a particular toy. Out of generosity, or more likely frustration, the parent buys the toy for the now happy child. But after only a few days, the toy very often will begin to lose its appeal, and soon, the child loses all interest in it and wants another new toy. As adults, we behave in exactly the same manner except our toys are more expensive. But the principle is the same: We are rarely satisfied. When we try to find happiness through ideas, possessions, or other people, we will never attain happiness because what we want to accumulate are, by their very nature, transitory and impermanent. Ideas change or go out of favor; possessions break, get lost, or are taken from us. People die or simply leave us.

All of us have greed, desires, and attachments for things, people, life, and more. Why? We are deluded, and in our unawareness we do not see things as they really are. It is like looking at the reflection of the moon in the water and thinking it is the real moon. We do not see the reality. We do not understand that we are one with the universe. We do not truly understand causality and why things happen. We do not understand that we are drowning in our selfishness and ignorance, or that everything is impermanent and constantly changing. We do not understand that life entails suffering, that it is caused by craving, that suffering can end, and that the way to its end is the path of proper practice.

Our lack of understanding is an underlying cause of why we are still unhappy, still discontent. Our lack of awareness blinds us to the truth. It is like being awakened by a strange sound in the night: In our ignorance, we think that it is an intruder and we panic. Upon realizing it is only a branch tapping against a window, we relax. In our ignorance, we do not know what is real. We thought the intruder was real and panicked, but we were wrong.

And if we think that we are individuals and that we have a self, we are again wrong. If we have a "self," where is it? Is it in our heart? In our mind? Somewhere else in our body? As Buddhists, we believe that there is no independent self. We are interrelated to everything in the universe. Until we realize this through our own experience, we will do everything we can to protect our "self," to make our "self" more comfortable, to keep our "self" alive longer—all because we do not yet realize that we are all one. We are still deluded, still ignorant. And ignorance gives rise to attachments, cravings, jealousy, bitterness, and more. When our greed is not satiated, we give rise to the heart of anger of which there are many forms.

When we do not get what we want, we become annoyed. When we lose what we have, we become resentful. When we are unable to be with people we like, we become irritated. These are all forms of anger. Anger has its roots in the discriminatory and mistaken idea of "I am an individual." As a consequence, we feel the need to protect our ideas and possessions, the need to protect who we are individually. Ignorance leads us to think in terms of gain or loss, of pluses and minuses, and so we feel the need to protect what is ours, whether it is a thing, an idea, or a person.

This concept of "mine" leads to selfishness, which in turn results in our wanting, either of what we do not have or more of what we already have. This is greed and when our greed is not satiated, we feel resentment and anger. When anger remains unchecked, it will intensify into hatred that inevitably grows stronger until killing becomes unavoidable—

all because of a flawed concept, all because of "I."

Greed that is not satiated results in anger. Greed and anger arise because we are ignorant and do not know that craving leads to more craving. This, the Buddha said is the second truth: Suffering is caused.

The Buddha did not just tell us what the problem was—that life entails distress, that our lives are filled with dissatisfaction, that we are unhappy much of the time—and then leave it at that. He went on and explained that this is caused by our own greed. This greed comes from our ignorance. And then he told us unequivocally that there is a way to end this suffering.

We can do this by eliminating our selfishness. When our greed and attachments no longer exist, suffering ceases, and the state of Nirvana is attained. Nirvana is the state in which we are permanently liberated from our unhappiness. In this state, there is no thought of "me" or "mine," and there is no more greed, anger, and ignorance. Instead, there is peace, love, wisdom, and a level of complete happiness that we cannot imagine or begin to describe.

The Buddha did not tell us about suffering to take the joy out of our lives. He did not intend that we should feel that life was depressing or unbearable or hopeless. He just wanted to shake us out of our complacency. He hoped that we would awaken and replace our current state of ignorance with one of understanding. To deny that suffering exists is pointless. But to become immersed in feelings of hopelessness is equally futile. We need to follow the Middle Path and find an inner balance, to neither drown in nor ignore distress, but to strive to overcome our unsatisfactory existence. Thus, we now realize the third truth: Suffering can end.

The way to its end is the fourth truth: Practice. Different traditions and teachers may explain the practice in slightly different ways, but the essence of practice is discipline, concentration, and wisdom.

THE PATH TO LIBERATION:
DISCIPLINE, CONCENTRATION, AND WISDOM

By acknowledging the existence and source of suffering, we can cease to create further unhappiness by practicing moral self-discipline. This enables us to attain the meditative concentration that gives rise to intuitive wisdom.

As with everything the Buddha taught, moral discipline, meditative concentration, and intuitive wisdom are not the result of his personal opinions or arbitrary judgments. They are derived from the standard of what is correct, honest, and beneficial. For example, to say that lying is wrong is not a personal opinion. It is morally wrong because it is deceitful. If we say something untrue or we simply exaggerate something, the other person will react improperly because we had given him inaccurate information. Lying is morally wrong because what we said was not correct and we were not honest. Also, lying is not beneficial to either the speaker or the listener. The seeds for being hurt in the future have been reinforced in the speaker, and the seeds for sadness or bitterness have been sown in the listener. These standards of whether something is correct, honest, and beneficial can enable us to develop discipline, meditative concentration, and wisdom.

To begin our practice we can start with some basic understanding. First, we can test to see if suffering exists, and if it is caused by craving and by expectations. When we experience events not going the way we anticipate, when good times do not last, when those we love are not always with us, and we feel that, yes, life is largely unsatisfactory, we are experiencing the reality of discontentment. But we cannot stop there.

For many, it becomes logical for one to want to embark on the path to genuine happiness. The Four Noble Truths are in themselves statements of causality. We have craving and expectations, which we anticipate will make us happy. If we were to just land this new job, or if only this wonderful person were to fall in love with us, life would be wonderful. But, when these desires are not fulfilled, distress arises. When we remain stuck in an old job, or there is no one to meet us when we go home at night, we undergo disappointment and loneliness because our expectations remain unfulfilled.

But what if we obtained what we wanted? Inevitably, things will become unsatisfactory when our other expectations, of which there are many, are not met. The new job requires us to work long hours and there are constant deadlines we have no hope of making. The wonderful person falls in love with us, but after a while we discover that he is not really that wonderful. Perhaps his habits are annoying or he does not really listen to us.

Thus, when our wishes and expectations are not met, unhappiness is created. And even when our hopes are fulfilled, the happiness will at some point begin to fade when our expectations change. Consequently, discontentment is created yet again. Inevitably, we end up unhappy and unsatisfied, if not from one thing, then from another, all because of expectations that arise when we have attachments and craving.

To reduce our craving and eliminate our attachments, we can practice nonattachment. Think of it as letting go. It does not mean withdrawing from society to lead a reclusive life. And it most certainly does not mean neglecting our responsibilities either. We still need to do the best we can in whatever we are doing, whether we are meeting that deadline at work or washing the dishes at home. The true spirit of letting go is the detachment from desires and expectations. It is our greed that creates suffering. When greed is reduced, discontent will likewise lessen.

If we keep telling ourselves that we want something because it will make us happy, we are reinforcing that desire and increasing our unrealistic expectations. Once we understand causality, we will realize that what we have now and will have in the future is what we have destined ourselves to receive, from what we did in the past. This happens whether or not we desire it. But with no desire, we avoid potential disappointments.

When we no longer have craving and expectations, we will not undergo disappointments due to our unfulfilled desires. Not being disappointed helps us to be happier. If something enjoyable happens, of course we appreciate it, for unexpected happiness is the best of all kinds of happiness. But more importantly, without expectation, there is no disappointment. How can we miss what we never thought of having in the first place?

Initially, in our practice of nonattachment, we will focus on relieving our own dissatisfaction by training ourselves to let go of attachments and expectations. Gradually, we will develop the wish to help those around us to also end their suffering. As we keep expanding this caring to others, we will be increasing our loving-kindness. No longer thinking solely of ourselves, we will seek happiness for all, and thereby practice compassion and not harm others. Eventually, our heart of loving-kindness and compassion will encompass all other beings.

Letting go transforms greed and attachment. Loving-kindness transforms animosity and bitterness, and harmlessness transforms inconsideration and cruelty. Greed, ill will, and thoughtlessness arise from ignorance and our failure to understand causality. We can eliminate our ignorance with wisdom. But where do we begin?

We begin with moral self-discipline, with training.

On a basic level, we abstain from (1) killing; (2) stealing; (3) sexual, or sensual, misconduct; (4) lying; and (5) taking intoxicants. On a broader basis, we behave in a moral and ethical way in everything we do. These five trainings will be covered in more detail in the section on the precepts; but I would like to touch on them briefly here in short.

By not killing, we revere all life, and have compassion and respect not just for other people but also for animals, insects, plants, and the earth which supports us. By our very existence, we are taking lives. As we walk, we step on insects. To produce the food we eat and the water we drink, millions of other animal and microbiological lives are destroyed. We cannot stop eating or drinking water, but we can make certain we do not waste anything. Understanding our impact on others, we can use what we need, but no more than that.

Not killing also has a more subtle aspect: We should not kill the seeds of goodness in others or harm another emotionally. While our thoughts and actions can be damaging to others, it is our speech that all too easily commits this offense. Our careless, sarcastic, or angry words can deeply wound a child, a loved one, or a friend. We need to use our speech wisely and speak from the heart that wishes to help others.

By not stealing, we respect the property of others. We do not take or use anything without permission of the owner. This seems simple enough, but this training also means that we do not take that book which is lying unclaimed in a restaurant. Neither do we keep the extra dollar that the clerk mistakenly gave to us nor do we take things from where we work for personal use.

By not committing sexual, or sensual, misconduct, we do not indulge in sensual pleasures, understanding that to do so not only increases our attachments and craving, but our discontent as well.

By not lying, we speak truthfully, understanding the power that our words can have. We choose our words wisely realizing that great harm can result from ill-considered, untruthful speech.

By not taking intoxicants, we do not take substances that affect our ability to think and behave clearly at all times, and that harm our bodies. Remaining clear-headed helps us to not harm others or ourselves.

The second component of proper practice is

meditative concentration. In meditative concentration, we focus our attention on whatever we are doing at the moment: working, playing a game with our children, listening to a friend or loved one, or chanting a Buddha's name. There are no distractions or worries, no doubts or drowsiness, no discriminations or attachments: We remain unaffected by our environment and maintain a calm, undisturbed mind. Initially, this state will bring joy and a sense of ease. Eventually, it will enable us to see things as they truly are.

We can think of our mind as a mirror, which reflects everything perfectly. But this mirror does not judge, nor is it attached to the object that is seen reflected in it. Whatever is in the mirror is reflected clearly and purely. We try to do the same in our practice of meditative concentration. The objective is to see what appears in the mind, but to not try to hold on to what arises. When we accomplish this, we will no longer be pulled in one direction one moment and then in another direction the next. When the thought passes, we will not miss it. Our mind will return to a calm and clear state.

In everyday life, we can concentrate on whatever

we are doing. We will be aware of what is happening around us but we will not be distracted or disturbed by it. In daily life, we can practice meditative concentration in everything we do, whether we are working, watering the garden, or driving our car. We choose the object or activity of our attention and then remain focused on it.

The more we are able to concentrate, the better our lives will become. As our awareness increases, we will make fewer mistakes. Our frustration will diminish and we will become happier. Our objective in this kind of concentration is to reach a level where we no longer worry about what happened yesterday or fear what may happen tomorrow. We will thus feel more secure. Also, when we no longer find ourselves being swayed by whatever thoughts or feelings that happen to arise, we will remain calm.

We also strive to attain meditative concentration in our Buddhist practice. Some methods require the guidance of a teacher, while others can be practiced on our own. On our own, we can concentrate on impermanence. This will enable us to understand that nothing remains the same, and that craving and ignorance keep pulling us back into unhappiness.

In the practice of concentrating on no self, we will realize that everything is interrelated. There is no you, no I; there is just one. This practice will help us to reduce conflicts with others and to no longer experience loneliness and alienation. Instead, we will know the unity of all beings.

The practice of concentrating on Nirvana will help us to find this ultimate reality. No longer will we feel that there is more to life than what we are experiencing at any moment and that we are missing out on something more meaningful out there.

The practice of concentrating on a Buddha's name will help us to become one with the perfect compassion, perfect happiness, and perfect peace that is the Buddha. As we realize that we are already one with the one who is perfect, we no longer feel that we are going to take the journey by ourselves. Initially, the goals of understanding ultimate reality and attaining perfection may seem far beyond our reach. But the path to reach them lies at our feet. Proceeding on it requires moral discipline, meditative concentration, and intuitive wisdom.

The final component of proper practice is intuitive wisdom. Intuitive wisdom is not an intellectual pursuit nor is it a measure of academic intelligence. It is insightful knowing and understanding, and it arises from within us when our minds are clear and calm.

Initially, when we start the practice of moral discipline, meditative concentration, and intuitive wisdom, our motives will be more self-centered. This is perfectly normal and a reasonable place to start from as we seek to improve ourselves, with the aim of improving our lives and, then, of freeing ourselves from suffering. Gradually we will begin to generate the wish to help others. While we focus on reducing our own feelings of dissatisfaction, we will make progress—which is obviously good. But we will really begin to strengthen our practice when we generate the aspiration to help all others along the path as well.

KARMA AND REBIRTH

When the Buddha spoke of various universal phenomena and eternal principles, he was teaching what he himself had learned through observation and direct experience. He taught that everything is impermanent, the existence of suffering, how it is caused, and how to end it. The way to end all that is unsatisfactory and painful in our lives is to follow the path of discipline, concentration, and wisdom. Practicing with diligence on this path, one can attain liberation from distress and unhappiness.

The Buddha also spoke of the law of causality: We reap what we sow. Good results in good, and bad incurs bad. We have created our lives and are thus responsible for them. Since we are the ones who have created our lives, we alone can change them. Understanding that unhappiness is caused by craving and expectations, we can begin to change our lives by eliminating these negative emotional habits. If we have no expectations of someone or of certain circumstances, we will not be subject to disappointment and will not react with annoyance or anger. And if we are not immersed in frustration and resentment, we can remain calm.

The law of causality is not a man-made law or a judgment by an external force that impinges upon our lives: Causality is a natural law, as natural as a ball bouncing back to me after I had thrown it against a wall. As the physicist Sir Isaac Newton said, every action must have an equal and opposite reaction. Simply put, we reap what we sow. Since causality is a natural law, there is no judge, jury, or ruling body that determines our consequences: Our past thoughts, speech, and actions determine our lives today. And just as our lives today are the result of our past, what we say, think, and do today will shape our future.

The Buddha explained that phenomena are created by the heart. If we speak or act with an impure heart, then suffering will follow us, as surely as a cart follows the oxen that pull it. If we speak or act with a serene heart, then happiness will follow us just like our shadow does.

For me, personally, the karmic explanation of why things happen has always made sense. It was what first drew me to Buddhism. It may not yet provide the answers you seek, but for me it did. Why do some people have such difficult lives while others seem to have everything they could ever want? Why is there so much unhappiness in the world? Do things happen randomly or is there a pattern to existence?

From a Buddhist perspective, the law of causality explains that things happen to us because of what we have done in the past. We are responsible for ourselves. Hence, we cannot blame another for the circumstances in which we find ourselves. Understanding this, we will gradually learn to stop blaming others, our environment, even our parents for what happens to us. The inequalities in life are due to our own past thoughts, speech, and actions. These result in the family that we are born into, the person we marry, the children we have, and even the environment in which we live.

Karma is an action or a combination of actions performed by us and which invariably produces results. These actions may be good, bad, or pure. Good karma leads to favorable results and rebirth in the higher realms of rebirth. Bad karma leads to bad results and rebirth in the lower realms of rebirth. Pure karma leads to enlightenment and enables one to transcend the cycle of rebirth.

Karmic actions can be created by an individual or jointly by a group. The consequent results can be good or bad and help to determine the future of the individual or individuals who created them. While the cause will always produce a result, when that result will occur cannot be predicted. If the right conditions do not manifest for a while, the result will lie dormant for as long as it takes those conditions to mature.

Regardless of the time frame involved, the causal link is clear. Thoughts of greed, animosity, closed-mindedness, and of pleasing ourselves at the expense of others will result in adverse consequences. Thoughts of selflessness, consideration for others, and understanding will lead to good results. Our goal is to eliminate the selfish and negative actions, and to increase the positive ones. At every instant in our lives, we can decide what we will think, say, or do in the next moment. But unfortunately, most of the time we do not consciously make such decisions, either because we remain unaware that we can or are not used to doing so, or, all too often, we are simply too lazy.

Our every action is preceded by a thought, but we are so preoccupied with ourselves and so distracted by the ceaseless bombardment of our thoughts that it would seem that we act without thinking. Too late we realize that, once again, we have acted automatically out of negative habits and, consequently, planted another harmful seed.

Everything we do plants a seed in our most subtle consciousness. All the seeds lie dormant, waiting for the proper conditions to mature. If we, as gardeners, plant a seed in rich soil where it will receive lots of sunlight, water it properly, and take care of it, that seed will grow. If we place the seed in a bag and store it in a cellar, nothing will happen. Likewise, all of the seeds in our consciousness are waiting for the right conditions—karmic versions of the soil, sunlight, and water—to mature. When the seed matures, the cause brings forth a result. But it does not end there.

Cause and effect is a continuous cycle. A cause

triggers a result. That result then becomes a new cause, which will trigger another result, and on and on it goes. This chain not only affects us but others as well. We do something and it affects someone around us. In their response to our action, they affect someone else. This creates a wave-like response of cause and effect that moves outwards in an ever-widening circle, just like what results when a single drop of water splashes in the ocean: The ripple effect results in all the other drops of water in the ocean moving.

Each of us has planted a combination of good seeds and bad seeds. Thus, within each of us lies the seeds for both loving-kindness and treachery, for both goodness and unwholesomeness, and for both toler-ance and animosity. Which ones mature today will depend on our individual conditions. It would be helpful to remember when we are tempted to criticize another for her disloyalty that it could have just as easily been us in her place. We have all planted the seeds for deception and aggression. If we had en-countered similar conditions, we probably would have acted like those we were about to criticize. So while we do not condone or dismiss their behavior, we must realize the need to have wisdom, to practice compassion, and to keep everything in a proper perspective.

This can also help us to value our "good karma," that which makes us intelligent, skillful, and wholesome, and to not deplete it. If we keep enjoying the wholesomeness we created without accumulating any more, we will eventually use it all up. Since goodness brings goodness, it becomes even more logical to practice what we learned of discipline, concentration, and wisdom. This is where we can use the standard of what is correct, honest, and beneficial.

This responsibility of taking the initiative to sow good seeds for ourselves does not apply only to Buddhists. The law of causality is a natural law, like that of gravity. Some may say that they do not believe in gravity, but if a person who believes in gravity and a person who does not believe in it both jump off a diving board, do not expect that only one will fall while the other happily floats around in the air. The natural law of gravity takes over, and it applies to all. They will both splash into the water. And just like the law of gravity, we are all subject to the law of causality. This should not be depressing but liberating, for it means we are not hopelessly stuck with our karma.

We can choose to nurture one group of seeds over another.

Sometimes we can see causality functioning around us. In the example of jumping off that diving board, the cause is the jumping and the result is falling into the water. At other times the link between a cause and its result is not as apparent. This brings us to another important concept that the Buddha spoke of: rebirth. This should not to be confused with reincarnation. Rebirth is the causal link from one lifetime to the next, as the most subtle level of consciousness passes from one life to the next, like a river flowing from one place to another. On the other hand, reincarnation is generally defined as the movement of the soul from one life to the next.

Reincarnation is not solely an Eastern concept. Pythagoras remembered his previous birth. Plato remembered a number of his former lives. Other western philosophers, such as Emmanuel Kant, have spoken of reincarnation. It has been reported that in the United States, thirty million people believe in reincarnation and a little over one half of its populace think it is a distinct possibility.

The Buddha experienced the reality of causality

and rebirth on his night of enlightenment. He not only saw his own lives but the lives of countless others as well. He later explained that on our long journey of life, as we wander aimlessly from birth to birth, there have been more tears shed for us than there is water in the oceans.

You may not believe in causality and rebirth, but regardless, like gravity, they will still be there and can provide answers as to why good people may undergo endless difficulties, while others who are selfish and uncaring enjoy great wealth and power. Causality and rebirth can also explain the existence of geniuses; for example, Mozart and Rembrandt, or why one child is loving and filial, while his sibling is deceitful and ungrateful. Mozart and Rembrandt may have been creative geniuses who had strong passions for their art and who found themselves again being pulled by that karma into a later lifetime where that talent resurfaced. And siblings are more a product of their own individual past karma than of their current environment.

Those who are undergoing difficulties, despite their current goodness, had created the causes for those difficulties in their past lives and, on rare occasions, earlier on in this lifetime. Now, the conditions for that person to undergo difficult consequences have matured. They are reaping what they sowed in the past.

Those who selfishly enjoy great wealth without practicing generosity in this current lifetime are coasting along on their positive karma that they had created in the past. But their current self-centered behavior will cause them to quickly run through that karma, like a person who keeps writing checks without depositing more money into the bank. At some point, because there are not additional causes that create wealth and good fortune, their current store of positive karma will be depleted, and suddenly they will begin to experience many problems.

We do not need to know what the exact circumstances are or what the precise cause and effect is. It is the proper understanding of the general concept of the law of causality that can help us to become better people, and this is what we need to focus on. Upon seeing those who are experiencing difficulties, we are wrong to simply dismiss them by thinking that their current adversities are the result of their own past actions, and thus the hardships are essentially their own fault. With right understanding, we will do the opposite. We will feel compassion for them and have the wisdom to know how to better help them.

What they did in another lifetime or even earlier in this lifetime has long passed from their conscious mind, or has been forgotten, just as our former actions are likewise long forgotten by us. This should hardly be surprising considering how little we remember of what we did only yesterday! Here and now, in this lifetime, people who are undergoing great difficulties feel that they are helpless victims, pulled this way and that by circumstances they seem unable to change or control.

We cannot just say that this is their karma and use this as an excuse to do nothing. For us to blame and dismiss them is to act out of ignorance and arrogance. Instead, knowing about the existence of suffering and causality, we can choose to be nonjudgmental and use compassion as we try to understand and help them. We can think about what they are undergoing and remind ourselves that if we do not wish to find ourselves in similar circumstances, we need to practice generosity, loving-kindness, and compassion.

THE THREE DHARMA SEALS

Every Buddhist teaching bears the Three Universal Dharma Seals. Without all three seals the teaching is not a Buddhist teaching. In the Mahayana tradition, the three seals are impermanence, no self, and no wish. Impermanence and no self belong to our world of existence, to our limited view of reality. The state of wishlessness—Nirvana—is the ultimate reality.

The first Dharma seal stresses that all fabricated things are impermanent. These include our thoughts and feelings, ourselves, our world, and everything around us. Our thoughts and feelings are in a constant state of flux. One moment we may be happily laughing and in the next miserable as something that is said deeply hurts us.

We are constantly changing: Our body cells are continuously regenerating themselves. We can see this in a general sense when we look in a mirror.

What we see in the mirror is not what we saw a year ago. It is similar, but not exactly the same.

Knowing that a flower will not be around forever, or that the person we love will no longer be with us one day will remind us to cherish our time with them and not take them for granted. Realizing that a wonderful moment will soon be gone will motivate us to appreciate it now. We do not want to regret later that we missed an opportunity because we thought that there would be another chance to enjoy it later.

Understanding that nothing is permanent will help us to accept the fact that people and the things we love will not be with us forever. We will thus value them even more. Also, knowing that everything changes, including unhappiness, gives us the hope that unpleasant circumstances may improve for the better, that negative conditions may later turn positive.

The second Dharma seal explains that nothing that exists has an individual self. When we look in that mirror, we perceive what we think of as "self." We look a little different than we did a year ago, but we perceive ourselves as being the same person. But once we think of "me," it becomes natural to think of "you" and "others." That is how discrimination, with all its inherent ills, starts. Eventually, we discriminate against everyone and everything. But "I" is composed of minerals and elements that used to be someone or something else. One hundred years ago, "I" did not exist. One hundred years from now, "I" will no longer be here, at least not in this form. Part of the physical "I" may be in a cloud, another part in a flower, or another part in a new book—no more "I."

At some time, each of us will die. If we understand that throughout the universe there is only one being and that we are therefore all part of one another, that we are not individuals, that our component parts will separate and re-form, and that our loved ones are already one with us, then we will not be overwhelmed with sadness when the physical separation occurs.

Hearing that nothing has an individual self might be very difficult to accept. Perhaps we can appreciate this concept more if we look at an example that demonstrates interconnectivity, such as pollution. To pollute the environment or to pollute one part of our body is to pollute and harm the whole of ourselves. When one organ in our body is nourished, polluted, or hurt, our whole body will be affected similarly.

Likewise, being part of a single, bigger entity, to nourish ourselves is to nourish all beings.

Understanding that there is no independent self and that we are all interrelated and part of one another will bring us a sense of togetherness and peace, while viewing ourselves as individuals can lead to feelings of isolation or superiority. If we feel we are separate from everything and everyone, we might be unable to connect with others and will become caught up in self-pity. On the other extreme, feeling that we are separate from others, we might begin to think that we know the best way to do things and that others are not as bright as we are. Feeling superior can lead to the justification that it is right to impose our views on others and that controlling others is justifiable.

The Third Dharma Seal is Nirvana, the state of wishlessness. Not a place or a state of nothingness, Nirvana is a state that is beyond suffering, beyond craving for worldly existence or sensual indulgence. It is the extinction of the ideas of self and other, birth and death, gain and loss. It is the cessation of thinking that I can attain happiness even though others have not or that the distress of others is their concern, not mine.

Understanding that the way to ultimate liberation is Nirvana, we will understand that genuine happiness is not to be found in a materialistic, self-centered existence. It is achieved through compassion, moral self-discipline, meditative concentration, and innate wisdom. Only by passing to a state beyond anything we can now imagine or attempt to describe will we truly be free and be able to help others to be free as well.

THE FOUR IMMEASURABLE MINDS

How can we help others to find happiness? One way is through the practice of the Four Immeasurable Minds. The first mind is that of loving-kindness, which is offering happiness to others. The second is the mind of compassion, which is the intention and wish to relieve the suffering of others. Third is joy, which is felt when beings experience happiness. And fourth is equanimity: being neither averse to nor attached to anything. We should understand that we cannot cause others to transcend suffering or to feel happiness or joy, but we can still have the wish that all beings will be able to accomplish such freedom and joyfulness.

Ideally, one day, we will naturally want to practice all four because of our love for all beings, but realistically, until that day, we need to start from where we are and from what we can relate to. Thus, our practice of the Four Immeasurables can begin with wanting others to be happy. Gradually this can progress to wanting them to attain joy. Happiness is a physical state; joy a mental one. The attainment of joy, as well as the wish for others to attain the state of joy, is a higher-level achievement, higher than the condition of physically feeling good.

We can start this practice with those who are closest to us: our family and friends. We can then extend it to those we know and like, and gradually keep on expanding this practice outwards until we feel loving-kindness, compassion, joy, and equanimity for all beings in our world, and eventually for all beings throughout the universe. Ultimately, the capacity of our mind to care for all beings becomes immeasurable. Then our mind embraces the expanse of space and encompasses the vastness of the universe.

These four stages are akin to how a fire grows from strength to strength. First, to start the fire, we need paper and thoroughly dry kindling wood. There must be no draft and we must carefully tend our fire, focusing on it completely. As it begins to burn more strongly, we can add larger pieces of wood, which in turn increases the fire. Eventually, when our fire is blazing intensely, even adding large logs that are not yet dry can still fuel the fire.

The first mind is loving-kindness. This is the practice of selflessness, where we constantly seek to benefit others and to help others to find happiness. When we wish to hurt another, we are experiencing anger. Waiting for an opportunity to inflict harm on that person, we are experiencing animosity. When animosity continues for a long time it becomes hostility. When we act upon these thoughts through speech or actions, the hostility becomes cruelty. To counter these destructive emotions, we need loving-kindness.

To offer happiness to others, we need to know what they want, and for this we need to listen and understand. If someone tells us that they do not need or want something but we insist on giving it to them, we are only offering frustration and irritation, not happiness. If they wish for nothing, then giving them nothing is the offering of happiness. We should try to give others what they wish for as long as it is not harmful, even if what they like is something we do not. Our personal desires or opinions simply do not always reflect what other people want.

So often in our wish to make others happy, we

project what we like onto them. Our intentions may be good, but without wisdom the best of intentions can backfire, exasperating others and disappointing ourselves. To offer happiness, we need to set aside the thinking that others wish for what we wish and, instead, provide other people with what they truly wish for.

The second mind is compassion, or the wish and intention to alleviate the suffering of others. It counters sorrow and anxiety. It is the unconditional care and concern for all living beings, the ability to realize that all beings experience distress, not just ourselves or those we care for. All too often we find ourselves trying to ease the pain of those we love and care for, but completely disregarding the pain of other people whom we do not care for or even dislike. Ideally, our compassion should be felt equally to all.

This practice can be very powerful. Many of us have someone in our lives who seems determined to cause us problems. For instance, this person might be a supervisor who asks us how we would do a certain task. We would spend time searching for the best way to accomplish the task and then present our recommendation. But inevitably, the supervisor would disregard our suggestion and do as he wishes. This can be extremely frustrating.

But if we take the time to look carefully, we might well see that our supervisor is, in turn, under a great deal of pressure from his supervisor who constantly loses her temper. Under the constant threat of verbal abuse when anything goes wrong, our supervisor will naturally do what he feels most safe with. He is someone who truly needs our compassion, for he is constantly worried about being criticized or embarrassed, especially in front of others. By understanding his true situation, we can begin to feel some compassion for his constant distress.

In this and other situations, we can try to have compassion by understanding how the other person is feeling. It is not necessary to have experienced exactly what they are going through, or to become immersed in the situation with them. We will accomplish nothing if we empathize so completely that we are unable to effectively help them. Instead, we need to remain clear in our thinking and reactions.

If someone is drowning, jumping in not knowing how to swim will not help. What we need to do is to save her from drowning. To do this, it is not necessary to experience the same situation as the one she is experiencing. We need to calmly find a way to fix the situation, using our own experience and wisdom to guide us.

The third mind is that of joy, which is wanting all beings to be free from unhappiness and being sincerely happy, without any trace of jealousy, when they accomplish this. Joy counters sadness. It is the state of great contentment and ease.

All too often, we wish to control others. We become irritated when they fail to behave as we wish. If others then praise them for their behavior, we become even more frustrated. But we should learn to feel happy for them. If the person is genuinely happy in what they have chosen to do and their actions have not harmed anyone, then, yes, we ought to feel joy for them.

The fourth mind is equanimity, which is letting go. It counters attachment and aversion. It is to stop clinging and to no longer judge or discriminate. It does not mean that we do not love. It means that we love equally and impartially, like a mother who loves all her children. Loving every one of her children, a mother's love for one child is not lessened. Loving all her children with equanimity does not mean she is indifferent to what her children feel or do. She simply loves them all unconditionally and without expectations.

Equanimity in love is non-possessive. It is like the sun shining on all beings equally. The sun does not differentiate, deciding to shine more on this person and less on that person. Neither does the sun cling to those it shines on. It shines on all it sees with warmth and brightness—equally.

When we can view everyone with equanimity, we will understand that people are who they are. If we expect them to conform to our ideals, we will smother them and destroy them. It would be much better to just accept people as they are, without any of our pre-conceived views and personal judgments. Our only wish should be for them to be free from suffering, and to be happy and filled with joy.

Developing the Four Immeasurable Minds requires much time, enthusiasm, and dedication. Although our Four Minds today may seem to be very small and narrowly focused, their gradual expansion to encompass the whole universe will bring us immeasurable joy.

THE FIVE PRECEPTS

Most people want to live a safe, healthy, and happy life. How do we proceed toward this ideal? The Buddha provided us with five precepts to guide us on our way to individual liberation. Not just for Buddhists, these precepts are basic to the major spiritual traditions and ethical teachings in our world today.

The first precept is to refrain from killing. It is not the principle itself that people disagree on but rather its interpretation. Some believe that abstention from killing only refers to not taking the life of another human being. Others feel that it is wrong to kill both people and certain animals, but all right to kill insects. Still others believe that to intentionally take the life of any living being is wrong. All these are interpretations of not killing.

In Buddhism, not killing is the reverence for all life and is founded on compassion. All animals fear death and experience pain when hurt. Understanding this, we can try to be mindful of everything that we are doing: We do not want to inadvertently kill or hurt another living being. For example, we can try to be aware of where we are walking so we do not carelessly step on living creatures. By keeping our homes clean we attract fewer insects and mice, which reduces the likelihood of having to deal with removing them. If we do have mice, we can use traps that capture them alive and then free them in a safe area.

Why go to all this trouble? Why not just kill them and be done with it? Isn't it natural to kill lower life forms like animals and insects? In our ignorance and arrogance, we incorrectly believe that we are superior to animals. But within every being is a true nature identical to that of all Buddhas. These enlightened beings have uncovered their true nature. Ours remain buried deep within us. When we finally awaken and uncover our true nature, we, too, will attain enlightenment and become Buddhas.

Since all beings have this nature, we are, by nature, equal to one another. Our lives are different due to the different causes we planted in our innumerable lifetimes. All these causes are stored in our most subtle consciousness. When certain conditions are right, certain causes will mature, bringing forth corresponding consequences while all the others will remain dormant. In this lifetime, the causes we planted to be the person we are have matured. The causes an animal planted to be born as that particular animal have likewise matured. Next time our roles could be reversed!

As we progress in our practice of compassion and no killing, the objective is not to give rise to a single thought of irritation, much less to anger. Compassion must be experienced and felt, not just understood on an intellectual level. Only when compassion and gentleness are an active part of our being will we stop reacting out of anger and hatred. Left unchecked, anger and hatred will eventually result in killing. Only when loving-kindness is a functioning part of us will we end the wars within and between each of us and attain peace for all.

Often when we are discussing the precept of no killing, people ask if all Buddhists are vegetarian. Actually, the Buddha never told us that we needed to be vegetarians. When he and those who were with him went into a town to silently request food, people would sometimes place meat in their alms bowls. So the Buddha ate meat when it was offered to him. But he did provide guidance as to when eating meat was inappropriate. Buddhists are not to eat meat if we see the animal being killed, if we hear the animal being killed, or if the animal is killed specifically for us.

Whether Buddhist practitioners choose to simply follow these three rules or whether they decide to become complete vegetarians often depends on environmental conditions and on specific cultural traditions. No matter what the reason is for not eating meat, many studies have concluded that vegetarians generally enjoy better health and live longer.

The second precept is to refrain from taking what is not given. By not taking anything without permission, we will be free of nagging thoughts of having done something wrong. Even if an object appears not to belong to anyone, taking it will break this precept. Not stealing also includes paying others a reasonable and fair wage for work that is done, treating others fairly in a business, and returning borrowed items in a timely fashion. Just as the deeper meaning of abstaining from killing is compassion, the deeper meaning of not stealing is giving.

The third precept is usually interpreted as refraining from sexual misconduct. But this precept is actually addressing any sensual indulgence: craving for food, sensations, and much more—not just sexual misconduct. Sensual indulgence distracts us from our inward search to find lasting happiness and freedom. It wastes our energy and leaves us with escalating wishes. We should not allow ourselves to be controlled by our senses; instead, we need to refrain from indulging our senses. This will help us to feel more in control of our lives, to be more self-confident.

The fourth precept is to refrain from telling lies. We should not deceive others for our benefit or for the benefit of those close to us. Instead of separating people with careless speech, we can use speech to bring others together, creating understanding and harmony.

Not lying also means that we speak at the right time and in accordance with the facts. We are logical and say what is useful. We do not gossip or boast. By following this precept, we will find ourselves using words that are correct, honest, and beneficial. This will stop us from creating negative consequences for ourselves. Because we are honest and thoughtful, we will have the trust and respect of others. And by not offending others or causing dissension, we will get along well with people.

In our practice of not lying, we need to also use wisdom and compassion. What should we do when a friend asks us how we like her new haircut? Or when you are driving to meet friends for dinner, and your husband asks if what he is wearing is okay. It is too late to do anything, and complete honesty will not be helpful at this point. It would be kinder to not say that the haircut is too short or that the shirt is an unbecoming color.

If our genuine intention is to avoid hurting the other person and not to flatter, then we can say the haircut and the shirt are fine. Afterwards, we can try to find a way to say that the former haircut was more flattering and, perhaps, the shirt is not very becoming. For this, we need to find the right time.

Precepts are not to be adhered to merely on a literal basis. We need to understand their logic, so as to better judge how to wisely follow them. If we understand the intention behind a precept, we will be better able to adhere to its inherent meaning when encountering challenging situations.

One good example of a precept that is easier to follow if one is aware of it's underlying purpose is the fifth precept of refraining from intoxicants. This precept is not universally held, but the Buddha gave it to us in the hope that we would not take anything that would impair our judgment or that would lead us to harm others or ourselves.

It is already difficult for us to abstain completely from killing, stealing, sexual misconduct, and lying. All of them encompass our thoughts, and verbal and physical behavior in some combination. Although we can usually manage to control our behavior to some degree, restraining our thoughts is more difficult. When impaired judgment and reflexes reduce our mental restraint, which is what happens when we indulge in intoxicants, then taking them can result in our heedlessly breaking other precepts.

Some people may ask, "What is wrong with drinking one glass of wine or having a beer with friends?" They may feel that it is okay and believe that one drink does not impair their judgment. But others might respond that this is setting a bad example for our children and those with us and that, ultimately, it impacts our ability to awaken.

Not smoking is also included under this precept. Studies are now indicating that smoking tobacco alters the brain in a similar manner to certain drugs, so smoking can actually impair our judgment. In addition, smoking is an addictive sensory indulgence, and addictions keep us from awakening and our goal of a pure mind.

We also need to be wary of the consumption of toxins in what we see and hear. The toxins of violence, hatred, and fear in television programs, movies, books, and the Internet are just as influential and damaging. We do not need to go to extremes on this; we just need to be careful in what we consume through each of our senses, and to make wise choices in what we read and view.

Precepts are not designed to prevent us from having a good time. They help us to find and develop the inner strength to think and conduct ourselves correctly. By knowing how to be more mindful in our thoughts, speech, and conduct, we will feel freer and less worried about behaving improperly or inadvertently hurting others.

THE SIX PARAMITAS

How can we get along better with others? What can we do to stop being so self-absorbed? And how do we, instead, develop the mind of compassion and joy? We can follow the examples of bodhisattvas, beings who are awakened, who no longer feel jealousy or sadness, and who are dedicated to alleviating the suffering of all beings by showing them the way to liberation. These beings practice the six paramitas, or perfections, of (1) giving, (2) moral discipline, (3) patience, (4) diligence, (5) meditative concentration, and (6) wisdom.

The first of the paramitas is giving. Giving counters greed, and ensures that in the future we will have ample resources to continue helping others. The underlying meaning of giving is letting go.

There are three basic kinds of giving. First, we can give material resources such as food, money, clothing, and so on. Just as important is to give of our-selves: our time, energy, or skills. Second, we can teach others what we know, should they wish to learn. Third, we can inspire fearlessness in others, which occurs when we relieve them of their worries and apprehensions.

The giving of wealth can be of material resources or our time and energy. What we have that others do not, we can freely give to them. When we see others with an urgent need, we can take the initiative and provide them with what they need, be it a material object or assistance in what they are doing. If we see someone who is without food, we can initially pro-vide them with food, and then try to find ways to help them become self-sufficient.

As our giving becomes increasingly unconditional, we will begin to feel more spiritually liberated. The more we give away, the fewer possessions we have to worry about. Soon, we will realize that we need very little to be truly content. For example, those with abundant wealth worry a great deal about protecting their possessions from theft and loss. After giving, we will find our worries reduced and our minds calmer.

Lacking material objects to give, we can give of our

abilities and energy. When we see others who need assistance, we can pitch in and help them. We do not need possessions or wealth to practice this kind of giving. We can just selflessly help others through our actions. But for some people, giving of themselves is more difficult than giving material objects. To be able to give of our time requires us to stop thinking of ourselves and to, instead, focus on someone else. For example, instead of watching a game on television, we might go outside and play a game with our children or help an elderly neighbor with some yard work. In addition, when we commit to doing something, we need to follow through on our promises. When we have difficulty giving of ourselves, we are falling back into selfishness. Initially, giving might seem daunting, but with practice it will become more spontaneous, and consequently, more liberating.

Teaching is another form of giving. By teaching others, we are helping them to learn how to rely more on themselves. We give material resources to try to solve immediate needs. But, if we want to solve needs that are more far-reaching, we teach. It is not necessary to have exceptional skills. We can simply teach whatever we are good at.

But when we teach, we should not hold anything back. Consider the situation where our supervisor tells us to teach a new employee our job. How many of us will hesitate? We might think, "If I teach this person everything, he will replace me. And what if I do not get promoted? I may lose my job! I think I will hold back some important information. This way I will stay indispensable and my job will be secure."

Or, we may be asked for our recipe to that wonderful lasagna we alone know how to bake. Along the same selfish lines, we might think, "If I teach this person how to make my lasagna, people won't rave about mine as much. I'll leave out an important ingredient. Then I'll keep my reputation as a wonderful cook!" This is not giving. This is selfishness. When others wish to learn, we should teach them everything we can. Only then is it genuine teaching.

In the giving of teaching, the highest form of such giving from the Buddhist perspective is teaching others about causality, about the truth of the existence of suffering and the way to end it, and the way to liberate oneself from the cycle of rebirth. Teaching others everyday skills will bring happiness, but it will be short-lived. Teaching others how to become self-sufficient, thereby making it possible for them to provide for themselves and their families, will enable them to have self-respect and to care for those they love as well as those who need help. But teaching others to be permanently free from suffering will bring them genuine and lasting joy.

The last kind of giving is that of fearlessness. This form of giving removes the insecurities, worries, and fears of others, whether the "other" is human or non-human. As humans, we are afraid of many things: losing those we love, being alone, becoming ill, dying. We worry that we will not be able to provide for our families and ourselves. We worry that we will not live up to the expectations of others and to our own self-image. When we see others who are likewise afraid or uneasy, we can help to alleviate their discomfort. The giving of courage can be the sharing of a kind word, the giving of our strength and stability, or our understanding. Even a simple smile is a form of the giving of fearlessness, since it can lessen another's fears. When we relieve the worries and fears of others, and help them to feel more secure, they will be able to find peace and self-respect.

Whatever we do, we should focus on that person.

When we act with absolute sincerity, the smallest act or a few encouraging words can work wonders to alleviate the apprehensions of others.

We can also give non-fear by helping wounded animals, by not participating in activities in which animals are harmed, and by reducing our consumption of meat and fish. Giving fearlessness is enabling all beings, not just humans, to feel safer around us. It is the practice of respecting all forms of life.

Whether we give material possessions or our time and abilities, we are practicing the giving of wealth. As Buddhists, we believe that those who have wealth now were generous in the past and those who give wealth now will have wealth in the future. If we teach others today, we will be wise in the future. By giving fearlessness, we will have long, healthy lives. The giving of intangibles—of fearlessness, of teaching, of our abilities and energy—costs us nothing, but it has the potential to change ourselves and to help others.

But if we give with some expected return in mind, then what we will be receiving will be limited. When we learn to give without thoughts of what we will receive, the return will be much greater because we will be giving from our true nature.

One of our major challenges to becoming awakened is greed, which results in clinging to things, people, and ideas. The best way to counter greed is through giving. Ideally, we would want to start with what is most difficult to give, but since this is very hard. for most of us, we can start more modestly. What is important is how we give. If we feel that we have made a sacrifice, then we have not truly given. Neither have we given if we constantly think of what we gave, or even wish that we still had it. We may have given in the physical sense, but mentally and emotionally, we are still clinging to the object. This is not true giving.

If, on the other hand, we spontaneously give something to someone just because it seems so right for her and will make her happy, and then we do not think of the object again, we will be practicing true giving. Initially, in our practice of giving, we will be happy that we have helped others. In time, we will naturally give without any thoughts of having given, of someone having received, or of what was given. At that point, we will feel the joy of acting from our true nature, the nature of perfect selflessness. The Buddha told us that in the ultimate state of giving to others, we will not to dwell on thoughts of having given, on what was given, or of the recipient. Ideally, upon giving, we let go physically, mentally, and emotionally. At first, this will be extremely difficult for us to do; but, gradually, we will cease to miss what we had given and then, at some point, we will even forget that we had given.

In the practice of giving, we need to give what will make the other person happy. To give thoughtlessly is not true giving. For example, it is not thoughtful to give our famous birthday cake to a person who is watching his diet. Telling him that he should just enjoy it because of the special occasion lacks consideration. If just a picture of a birthday cake will make him happy, then we should give the picture and forget about the real cake.

The manner in which we give is also very important. We should not give in a way that embarrasses the recipient or increases our sense of importance. It should not matter whether we like or dislike the recipient. We are to give nonjudgmentally and without differentiating between those we like and those we do not. When we say that we will give something, we should do so as soon as possible and not purposely make the other person wait. Also, we should not expect the other person to feel indebted to us.

There is no point in holding on to our extra possessions; after all, possessions are ours for a relatively short time. Give freely now, according to our abilities, and enjoy the goodness and joy that our generosity brings to others. We really need very little for ourselves. Once we have provided for our families and met our personal responsibilities, we can practice giving to relieve the suffering and unhappiness of others.

The second paramita is moral discipline, which counters worry and unhappiness, and enables us to continue on our way to awakening. In a more literal sense, it means abiding by the precepts, which, for Buddhists, can refer to the five precepts, the bodhisattva precepts, or the monastic precepts. In a broader sense, the second perfection means ethical behavior, such as following the customs and laws of wherever we are. Initially, as we begin our practice of discipline, we can focus on refraining from harming others. Gradually, we will begin to develop and increase our virtue. The ultimate form of this practice is to benefit others.

Properly practicing moral discipline requires us to use good judgment and wisdom to determine what is appropriate or inappropriate. By allowing ourselves to be led by our desires and acting impulsively, we can easily harm others and ourselves. Actions that benefit others now and in the future are appropriate; actions that bring only short-term benefit but which harm others in the future are inappropriate.

Exploiting our natural resources, such as by carrying out widespread deforestation without making provisions for the planting of new trees, is one such harmful action. Also inappropriate are actions that are done to benefit solely ourselves, especially those at the expense of others.

To guide us in our cultivation of non-harmful behavior, we can observe the Ten Virtuous Conducts. These are divided into three major categories: physical, verbal, and mental. Physically, we are prohibited from killing, stealing, and engaging in sexual misconduct. These have been discussed in the previous chapter on the five precepts. Verbally, we are prohibited from lying, using harsh speech, divisive speech, or enticing speech. Mentally, we are prohibited from giving rise to thoughts of greed, anger, and ignorance.

Lying is deceptive and dishonest. We need to speak only truthful and thoughtful words. The Buddha said:

> If you know anything that is hurtful
> and untrue, do not say it.
> If you know anything that is helpful
> but untrue, do not say it.
> If you know anything that is hurtful
> but true, do not say it.
> If you know anything that is both helpful and true,
> find the right time.

We lie because we are attached to our ideas, possessions, and other people. We "modify" the truth to protect our self-image. We "embroider" the truth and make things sound better or worse than they are because we want to be praised by others, or perhaps because we are afraid of appearing incompetent. We do not value the truth in our speech because we are ignorant and do not yet understand the consequences of our untruthful words.

If we wish to practice thoughtful and caring speech, we do not use abusive speech like shouting, nor do we use bad language. To speak harshly to others can destroy their peace of mind and that of all those who are around us. We also do not waste our time gossiping about others or discussing trivial matters. It would be much wiser to use that time engaging in activities that increase our peace of mind, like going for a walk, watching the clouds float by, sitting quietly in meditation, or chanting a Buddha's name.

We also need to refrain from divisive speech. This is when, for example, while we are speaking with one person, we tell him that someone else said something untrue about him. Then, while talking to the other person, we say the first one criticized her. We have spoken divisively and without realizing it sown the seeds for conflict.

Instead of using words to deceive others, we can ask ourselves if what we are about to say is correct, honest, and beneficial to the other person. To accomplish this, we need to be aware of what we are saying. If we are mindful of our speech, we will not carelessly say something incorrect, untrue, or harmful. If we are paying attention to what we are saying and to how the listener is reacting, we will be able to see if we upset or irritated the person. We will then be able to stop before we make the situation worse. Instead of creating more conflict and pain in this world, we will be able to foster harmony and promote mutual cooperation as we develop the patience to know when to speak wisely or when to simply remain silent.

In all of our speech, we can stop ourselves from harming others by refraining from using self-serving, careless, or inappropriate language. Usually, we speak without first thinking about what we are about to say or how it will affect others. We should try to remember to use the standard of what is correct, honest, and beneficial to judge what we are about to say.

The Buddha told us that speech karma is one of our most commonly committed offenses; and thus our speech karma creates more problems for us. While our thoughts do affect others, they are subtler, and thus the karmic consequences are lighter. And while we may think of doing something, the opportunity to physically act on the thought may never present itself. So, we have natural roadblocks in the creation of physical karma. But speech karma is so easy to commit. We simply open our mouths and all the unkind, thoughtless, and angry words come tumbling out. Speaking is so easy, but also so potentially harmful.

Our physical and verbal behavior, the first and second components of the Ten Virtuous Conducts, can be good or bad depending on our thoughts, which is the third component. It is our thoughts, which usually arise from varying degrees of greed, anger, and ignorance that are the precursors of our behavior.

Greed—our craving for material things and pleasant experiences, and much more—comes from our preoccupation with self. What begins as self-preservation, our need to meet basic requirements of shelter, food, and clothing, quickly expands to our desiring that which we do not need and more of what we already have. We equate the accumulation of things with happiness and success, and so fall into a cycle of wanting, obtaining, and more wanting.

Anger, like all negative emotions, seems to happen so naturally and spontaneously. Initially, we do not even notice it. It feels so normal to us—the emotions of being angry, being irritated, and being displeased. It happens so quickly that we hardly notice the rising rage. But before every action we commit and prior to every word we speak, there is a preceding thought. In our lack of mindfulness, we do not notice the thought of what we are about to say or do. If we can catch the thought as it arises, we will be able to refrain from acting out of anger. Ideally, by having a heart of loving-kindness, compassion, joy, and equanimity, we will stop anger from arising.

Why is it so important to eliminate our anger? Might not the expression of our anger get it out of our system, so to speak? No, because voicing or acting on our anger does not eradicate it. On the contrary, it leads to even more anger.

Our anger with a particular person goes back a long, long time—as Buddhists, we believe it goes back over uncountable lifetimes. Most of the time when we are speaking with another, we fail to be mindful of what we are saying. We may carelessly say something and hurt another's feelings without realizing it. In so doing, we have just contributed to planting another seed of anger in the consciousness of the other person.

The recipient of the angry outburst may not think anything of it, at least not until we meet again, and that seed matures. This next time the other person will say something to us with just a slight trace of animosity. Again, this incident is registered in both our consciousness. This enmity is passed back and forth each time our paths cross, and each time it increases and grows more serious. At some point it will turn into hatred. Eventually that hatred will explode and one of us will lash out at the other physically.

This is why voicing our anger to eliminate it does not work. It only allows the anger to grow. Anger is not to be acted upon, but faced, acknowledged, understood, and then released. When our anger and our self-centeredness are gradually reduced, we will get along better with others and we will begin to find our hearts of loving-kindness, compassion, and joy.

If you want to see the proof of this, look carefully into the face of someone who is always angry. Then gaze upon a person who is serene. Decide which one you would like to look like, which one you would like to be.

As we improve in our practice of discipline, we will gradually lessen what the Buddha called the three poisons of greed, anger, and ignorance, which we all have to some degree. If left unchecked, this greed and anger of ours will grow and spread, eventually consuming us. Not understanding what is happening, we allow this to happen because we are ignorant. This ignorance is not the lack of intelligence or a derogatory comment about someone's abilities. Ignorance is a lack of understanding of the underlying truths of what is happening to us and around us.

It is not knowing, or, perhaps, not believing in causality or in the impermanent nature of everything that is created. It is believing that we exist independently of everything around us, rather than realizing that everything is interdependent. It is thinking that happiness comes from outside of us: that it lies in other people, possessions, or ideas. It is the belief that it is okay to differentiate between those we like and dislike, that it is correct to look out for ourselves at the expense of others, and that it is reasonable to judge others based on personal opinion and not on facts.

When we think and act from ignorance, it becomes inevitable that we will make mistakes and not know how to fix our problems. As we begin to replace our ignorance with understanding, we will find that our greed and anger slowly dissolve. This is how we can get along better with others, become less self-absorbed, and develop the mind of joy.

The third paramita is patience, which counters anger and hatred, and helps us to avoid arguments and to achieve our goals. We need patience in almost everything we do. In school, we need patience to persevere in our studies. At work, patience helps us to properly accomplish our tasks. At home, patience is the foundation for interacting well with family members. Patience enables us to get along more harmoniously with those around us. It allows us to recognize our bad habits and to improve ourselves by changing those habits.

Practicing patience gives us the courage and inner strength to act wisely in the face of adversity. It allows us to remain unruffled, to understand why things happen, and to stop blaming others for our problems. It is the ability to stay with a difficult and challenging undertaking without complaining, being disappointed, feeling resentful, or giving up prematurely.

What is the biggest challenge to patience? Anger. When difficulties arise, we are usually surprised and without thinking of what we are about to do, we often act out of anger. This goes against the essence of the Buddha's teachings, which is not only to avoid doing harm but to provide help as well. In anger, we lash out at others, harming everyone and everything around us—as well as ourselves. Nothing is resolved. No one is helped. Instead, we create more causes for anger in our future, add to the suffering of others, and lose the opportunity to help another being.

The harmful effects of impatience, intolerance, and anger can still be understood even if you are not yet able to fully consider the suffering of others before your own. When the fire of anger burns within, our face literally becomes red, our features become contorted, and our enraged demeanor upsets others. We cannot sleep, find relief, or calm down. Friends and acquaintances avoid us. Even those who love us leave. We are alone. All because we gave in to anger.

We have a choice here. We really do. We do not have to allow this to happen. Whether we are an awakened being or, more likely, simply an ordinary person who dreads the feeling of losing her temper again, we can make a commitment to ourselves, a commitment to the practice of patience. Obviously, this is extremely difficult to do at first. We will have to keep reminding ourselves how anger feels and

what it looks like, and then contrast it with how serenity feels and appears to others.

First, we objectively consider a recent time we
were angry and then remember how we felt at that
time. Next, we remember the feelings of contentment and serenity that we experienced when we
were enjoying time with our family or good friends,
or perhaps a time when we were taking a walk on a
sun-drenched day in the fall or listening to some
soothing music. Finally, we choose to commit to the
cultivation of patience. This is done consciously and,
ideally, continuously. So often, our anger is automatic. Something happens and in our mindless reaction, we are instantly angry. The only way to counter
this is to remain in a continuous state of patience.
Also, we can tell ourselves that everything is impermanent. This not only applies to enjoyable situations
but to those that are difficult as well. Painful, trying
times will at some point end. This will happen much
more quickly if we do not keep fueling the fire with
our anger.

Instead of becoming angry in all those infuriating
situations, what can we do? We can remind ourselves that our reactions do not need to be blindly

automatic. We can choose how to respond. If it is already too late and we have lost our temper, we can remind ourselves that we can still alter the situation. Explaining away our erratic emotions by telling ourselves that we are right and are therefore justified in getting upset accomplishes nothing. Instead, calm down and talk to the other person. This way, we will have a chance to resolve the problem. To be happy, we just need to let go of our unhappiness.

What do we do when we are faced with a situation where calm logic and not retaliating with more anger just seem to make the situation even worse? One way is to withdraw and try to find a better time to talk with the person. Even when we manage to reach a more advanced state in our cultivation of patience, where we can remain calm in the face of someone's frustration and anger, we are not helping them if we remain there fueling their pain and, thus, their suffering. There is enough misery in the world already. Withdraw and try to determine what we have done to contribute to the situation. Next, sincerely determine how not to repeat the mistake. Then, find the right opportunity to talk calmly with the other person.

To act out of anger is to act violently. But we have been discussing how to find happiness. When does violence make a reasonable person happy? Never. Reasonable people only wish for happiness and goodness. Through giving and ethical behavior, we can create much joy. But it takes the cultivation of patience to safeguard this goodness, and protect it from the fires of anger and violence.

Practicing ethical behavior may result in our beginning to feel restricted by rules and requirements. If we approach our practice from an incorrect perspective, it might well seem rigid and forbidding. So, to help us avoid this problem, the Buddha wisely taught diligence, the fourth of the six paramitas.

Diligence, or enthusiastic effort, is the joy that we bring to our practice and to all that is worthwhile in our lives. It is the true delight that arises from deep within us when we are doing what is wholesome. It enables us to keep going when we feel tired or overwhelmed. It is refreshing and inspiring. Cultivating enthusiastic effort counters laziness and brings joy to our lives as we feel a sense of accomplishment, of finishing what we start.

Laziness is often revealed as procrastination. We

become involved in trivial activities and eventually end up in low spirits when the results disappoint. We know we have to do something but somehow we keep postponing it, or we allow ourselves to be distracted. For example, it suddenly becomes vitally important to move the flowers on the dining-room table to a slightly different position. After completing this "critical task," we sit down to what we are supposed to do. In a few moments, we remember that the bookshelf urgently needs rearranging—another "crucial" accomplishment. We again sit down but then decide that we should call a friend and tell him all about the new employee at work.

After several more such "essential" activities, the time that we had allocated to do our original task is gone. When we think of what we needed to do and what was actually done, our mood sinks. We do not feel any real sense of satisfaction from completing those ad-hoc tasks that we had deemed to be "crucial," for what we actually wanted to do remains unfinished. As we think about it, the original task still looms before us and now seems insurmountable. We become upset with ourselves for procrastinating and feel despondent because the task still needs to be done. Lacking energy, we feel defeated and disappointed. At this point, we might turn on the television and begin flipping from one channel to another or engage in some other pointless activity. These are all forms of laziness.

So how do we counter laziness? Through a commitment to what we feel is important and enough enthusiastic effort to see it through to completion. Picture again the scenario on task avoidance. You are lying on the sofa and flipping channels. The telephone rings and it is your supervisor. He asks if you could go to dinner in thirty minutes to discuss a promotion to become head of your department and a doubling of your salary. Would you still feel lazy? More than likely, you would be overflowing with enthusiasm and elation as you rush to dress for dinner!

What we tell ourselves about any given situation will determine our reaction to it. If we persuade ourselves that we have plenty of time to do something, that it is not that important, and that it can wait until tomorrow or next week, then we are foolishly wasting time. The Buddha once asked a student how much time a person has left. The student answered, "A few more days." The Buddha prompted him to think again. The student pondered the question further and then replied, "A few hours." "Think again," encouraged the Buddha. "A breath?" "Excellent." All we can count on is this moment—we cannot afford to waste time.

This realization is not meant to be depressing but encouraging. When we waste time, we usually feel uncomfortable as we compare our plans to the reality of what was accomplished. Perhaps we had told someone what we wanted to do, and they were depending on us to do so. Our laziness and procrastination may result in a friend being disappointed, a child or spouse being made to wait while we try to do something at the last minute, or a co-worker having to work harder to make up for our missing a deadline.

Previously, the question was posed of how we can attain happiness, find love, and receive others' respect. We cannot attain them through laziness. Neither can we attain liberation from suffering by being lazy. We need enthusiastic effort, perseverance, and dedication in our practice and in everything that we do. To develop enthusiastic effort, we must overcome laziness with right thoughts and understanding that will engender proper attitudes and a correct frame of mind.

With our personal relationships, try to remember how we were feeling when we disappointed our spouse or children. Or think of how supremely important they are to us, or more crucially, how important we are to them. With our work, we can focus on the seriousness of not being a dependable employee or employer. With our practice, we can come to the realization of the value of the opportunity to practice and understand the consequences of wasting yet another lifetime. These and similar techniques will gradually help us to discover how to counter our negative habits.

Having reduced or even overcome laziness, we may find that we still indulge ourselves in trivial activities. We still enjoy flipping between television channels, having long conversations with friends or co-workers about other friends and co-workers, and countless other nondescript activities. Such trivial activities, by themselves, are not intrinsically wrong. They harm us only because they distract us from accomplishing goals that we have set for ourselves: to be more caring of those we love; to cultivate loving-kindness, compassion, joy, and equanimity; to help others; to be more patient; and much more.

Enthusiastic effort brings joy to our lives as we feel a sense of fulfillment in finishing what we started. Trivial activities can feel like worthwhile activities if we are not careful. They will distract us from finishing what we started and rob us of the joy that comes from such accomplishments.

How do we determine whether an activity is worthwhile or trivial? We can ask ourselves what is the intention or the motivation for what we are doing. If the motivation is to help others and to enable them to find true happiness, then our time spent enthusiastically in perfecting our skills that will bring them joy is commendable. But if our intention is solely to benefit ourselves, then, in spite of our hard work, we are not truly practicing enthusiastic effort, no matter how eager and enthusiastic we are.

To bring happiness to others, we need to understand the causes of suffering and unhappiness. We ourselves need to be disciplined and patient. Once our hearts and minds know gentleness and peace, our verbal and physical behavior will change. Gradually, the peacefulness that is increasing within us will be reflected in what we do.

The Buddha explained that every living being has the same true nature—the same ability to awaken and become enlightened. The Buddha was once like us: an ordinary person who underwent the sufferings of birth, old age, sickness, and death. But he learned how to liberate oneself from suffering. How did he do this? He sincerely developed the aspiration to leave suffering behind and to lay aside unwholesome thoughts. He was determined to live a life of not harming others. A life of helping others. A life of discipline, understanding, and patience.

After he had attained supreme enlightenment, he explained that it took him innumerable lifetimes to reach the point where he was one night away from enlightenment. He arrived at that point through many practices of perfection. One of them was the practice of enthusiastic effort. How did he progress? One step at a time—just as he did, we can too.

The fifth paramita is meditative concentration. Our practice and training in discipline and not harming others will enable us to lessen our harmful verbal and physical behaviors and eventually end them. Our minds will become calmer and less agitated. When our minds are thus settled we will be better able to concentrate.

Our concentration will initially reduce and, then, gradually eliminate our negative thoughts and emotional behavior. We will then gain meditative concentration, which will enable us to uncover our innate wisdom. Thus, discipline, meditative concentration, and wisdom work together and are complementary.

Developing concentration counters our myriad wandering thoughts and helps us to focus. We become less easily distracted by others or circumstances. We begin our practice by calming the mind and focusing our attention on one thing for a certain length of time. In everyday activities, we can practice concentration in whatever we are doing.

Most of us have experienced being totally absorbed in a task we enjoy very much. Before we began the activity we might have felt tired, but as soon as we became engrossed in the activity our weariness dissolved. Or we might have been hungry before we started, but that too passed unnoticed. At some point someone or something interrupted us, and we were surprised to see that so much time had passed.

This is concentration, a state of single-mindedness that has few distractions. There are no worrying thoughts and no thoughts of time or of where we are. Due to our focused attention and the reduction of aimless wandering thoughts, this is a state in which we may even feel more energetic than before we began. By becoming calm and focused, anyone can achieve this concentration, and thus develop a serene and stable mind. We can use concentration in many activities at work and at home, and with family and friends.

To help us attain a more spiritual state of concentration, there are many things we can focus on: a flower, the sound of a bird, our breath, Amituofo—the name of a Buddha. Each of these can help us find varying degrees of peace and happiness. Whatever type of meditation we practice, we will find that we will benefit much more if we practice to attain a specific goal, such as one befitting our Buddhist practice.

Where is a good place to deepen our practice of concentration? Where we can live a simple but contented life without being distracted by frivolous activities or unnecessary sense stimuli, as these will just distract us and deplete our energy. We also need good friends who will properly support us and patiently help us discover our shortcomings, friends who are committed to achieving the same goals we are. What are the personal criteria for such practice? A wholesome lifestyle that does not harm others, enthusiasm and joy in what we undertake, honesty in everything we do, and a sincere determination to seek liberation for others and ourselves.

Our practice of meditative concentration will lead us to the last of the six paramitas, wisdom. Wisdom counters ignorance, and enables us to know how best to help others and to improve ourselves, including our ability to get along well with others. This wisdom is not that which is gained through intense study and analysis of many diverse subjects. That would be seeking wisdom from external sources. The wisdom that we are speaking of is intuitive wisdom.

The Buddha experienced this intuitive wisdom after he sat down on a cushion of grass, lightly closed his eyes, and entered a state of meditation. As he went deeper and deeper into that meditative state, he left study, analysis, and his previous practice of deprivation behind him. He went deep within himself and reached the state where he saw the reality of what was happening within him, around him, and throughout the universe. He finally experienced the true and complete reality, arising as it did, from deep within him. By attaining a serene and stable mind, he was able to achieve single-minded concentration. Undistracted by external conditions and no longer disturbed by emotions or pointless thoughts, he eliminated the poisons of the mind and uncovered what he, for innumerable lifetimes, had been seeking: Perfect wisdom. He reached it and entered it.

This wisdom enabled him to realize that there is no independent self, and that everything is part of one entity. Causality of any event in one being's life has the potential to affect the causality of beings throughout the universe, just as the movement of one drop of water in an immense ocean will result in the movement of every drop of water in that ocean. We are all one. When we look across the room and see that person whom we are so angry with and whom we almost wish to strike, it is the same as being very angry with ourselves and wanting to hit ourselves.

Does our left hand become angry with our right hand? Do they fight over who will open the door we wish to go through? Do they debate which one will pick up a cup of coffee? Does something belong to my left hand but not to my right? We can see and understand the absurdity of such dualities. But our understanding stops there. We do argue with the person who is standing next to us. We do fight over who will be first. We do debate the use of and the ownership of possessions. We see dualities between ourselves and everyone else because we are far from understanding. We have not yet touched our true wisdom.

Lacking wisdom, we look at reality but do not see it. It is as if we are viewing it through a tiny blurred window. We think that we see the whole truth. Another person looks through his tiny blurred window and is equally convinced that he has seen the whole truth. Although what we each see is different, and therefore results in different viewpoints, we are each convinced that we alone are right. We debate, argue, and fight. Convinced of our infallibility, we may even kill for our beliefs. If only we had just communicated better and shared what we each had seen through our respective windows, we might have understood a little more.

But without wisdom, we each view our tiny distorted piece of reality and take it for the true state of reality. We think we perceive the whole truth through our five senses—our eyes, ears, nose, tongue, and body—as we see, hear, smell, taste, and touch our tiny piece of reality. We automatically conclude what we perceive to be the complete and true reality.

As a result, all of our thoughts are based on blurred bits of reality, misperceptions of what we mistake for the complete truth. Our basically flawed conclusions lead us to discriminate, thereby developing a sense of ego or self. We think that "I" refers to ourselves, that "you" refers to another person, and that "they" refers to everyone else. We begin to judge others and find most of them wanting. Those we like or love, we praise as good; others we dislike or hate, we condemn as bad. We do not truly care about the people and things that fall in between.

We have expectations, and when they are not met, we suffer disappointment. But when they are met, we develop new expectations as the situation changes. We become emotionally attached and cling to those we love and things we like. We find disturbing and repellent those people and things we hate and dislike. We are never completely content. Going through life with all its ups and downs feels like an emotional roller coaster. Even when we find ourselves thinking that life is good, we sense that we might be at a peak and worry about plummeting down once again.

We put others and ourselves through this emotional roller coaster because we have not yet uncovered our wisdom. Perhaps we were fortunate enough to have touched this insight for a brief moment—when our minds were serene and stable, when our thoughts were on benefiting others, and when our enthusiasm and joy were strong within us. In that one instant, we had a glimmer of what was correct, honest, and beneficial. But, in a flash, it was gone again.

Everything we need is already within us. We have been talking about finding happiness and love. We have been searching with our senses—looking for happiness and love, listening for them, trying to breathe in, savor, or touch them. But that has not worked. Upon closer proximity, what we thought was happiness and love was just a temporary sense indulgence, not the real thing. They did not last. It was as the Buddha said: a drop of dew, a flash of lightning,

One minute, they are in our hands. The next instant, they are gone. Why?

In our ignorance, in our lack of understanding of what is really happening, we look for happiness, goodness, and peace in the wrong places. They are not outside somewhere waiting for us to find them: They are inside of ourselves. They are in the heart of every being. They are the same in every being. Happiness, goodness, and peace are who we really are. They are our true nature, our Buddha-nature. How do we find our true nature? Unconditional giving, moral training, deep-felt patience, and enthusiastic effort will enable us to develop meditative concentration. With meditative concentration, we will touch our innate wisdom. If we begin to practice these six paramitas in even just some small measure every day, starting with today, gradually, we will begin to look in the right direction, and eventually we will awaken to the perfect goodness, perfect contentment, and perfect joy that are already within our true nature, our Buddha-nature.

TAKING THE THREE REFUGES

At some point in our learning and practice, we will likely wish to formally commit ourselves to the Buddhist path. To do this, we take refuge in the Three Jewels of the Buddha, Dharma, and Sangha. When we do so, we are not taking refuge in someone or something outside of ourselves. The Three Jewels represent virtues that are already within each of us; thus, taking refuge in the Three Jewels is to return to the sanctuary of our own true nature, to our own innate virtues and goodness.

When we take refuge in the Buddha, we are leaving blind faith and delusion behind us as we seek to awaken and uncover the true nature within us. The Buddha was an ordinary man who attained supreme enlightenment. He wisely understood the causes of pain and unhappiness, and compassionately showed us the path he had taken so that we too might break free from suffering.

Each of us has the same true nature as the Buddha. Each of us has the potential to look within and return to that true nature. The choice to do so is entirely up to us. To take refuge in the Buddha is to make a commitment to ourselves, to our inner Buddha-nature. That commitment says that we will do everything we can to awaken and to uncover the inner goodness, compassion, and wisdom that lie deep within us.

When we take refuge in the Dharma, we are returning from incorrect views to right views and correct understanding. Our present lack of awareness and proper comprehension have obstructed us from seeing the reality of life and caused us to look at everything in a distorted way, as if we were looking at things through a tiny blurred window. When our minds become pure and our misconceptions are replaced with right understanding, we will give rise to wisdom and be able to see everything clearly. Since sutras are records of the Buddha's teachings and describe the truth of the universe, we can use the sutras as guidelines. If our thinking coincides with what is in the sutras, then our comprehension is correct.

Only when we clearly see the whole can our viewpoints and understanding be wise. The teachings of all Buddhas flow from their true natures. They teach us how to let go of benefiting solely ourselves, to attain purity of mind, to see life clearly, and to become enlightened. Upon hearing the teachings, we should be respectful and remind ourselves to cultivate right understanding and proper views.

When we take refuge in the Sangha, the community of those who practice the teachings, we are returning from pollution and dissension to purity of mind and harmony. As we associate with those who practice understanding and loving-kindness, and who feel and practice as we do, we will begin to learn from them.

Currently, our minds, spirits, and bodies are impure. The Buddha taught us that everything is a reflection of the mind. Everything therefore arises from the mind; in other words, from our thoughts and feelings. When our minds begin to clear, allowing us to see and understand why things happen, we will stop judging others and cease wanting them to meet our expectations. We will gradually find contentment with what we have. As we interact with others and handle situations more harmoniously, we will begin to be content with who we are.

Sincerely taking refuge in the Three Jewels will help us restore the perfect wisdom and virtues of our true nature so that we can attain clarity, freedom, and genuine happiness.

It is best to take the Three Refuges with a monastic who you think will be a good mentor to you: someone whom you can learn from, seek assistance from, and be associated with. If, however, you have no access to a monk or a nun, you can take the refuges yourself as an alternative. When you take the refuges with a monk or nun, remember that he or she is simply passing on the vow to you and serving as a witness. You are not taking refuge in that individual.

I am often asked why I became a Buddhist, why I took refuge in the Three Jewels. Buddhism is logical and, for me, it feels right. The Buddha himself exemplified compassion, joy, and equanimity; thus, he practiced what he taught—he was honest. He advised us not to blindly believe anyone but to consider carefully what that person is saying—he was open-minded. He spoke of ending the wars within each of us to find peace without—he was insightful. He taught that our lives are the result of what we had previously thought, said, and done—he experienced, espoused, and epitomized the reality of the oneness of the universe. Ultimately, the reason that the Buddha's logical approach feels right for me is that Buddhism appeals to my innermost nature, what I now realize is my Buddha-nature.

Pure Land Buddhism

The next question that I am often asked is what school I practice. My practice is the Pure Land school of Mahayana Buddhism, which is widely practiced in Asia. Though still in its formative years in the West, its roots extend all the way back to ancient India.

We generally think in terms of only one Buddha: Sakyamuni, who lived about 2500 years ago. But, since any sentient being can awaken and innumerable numbers have, there are innumerable Buddhas. Sakyamuni Buddha, after his enlightenment, explained that he saw not only his past lifetimes but also how the future would unfold.

Sakyamuni saw people in our time having more afflictions, worries, and wandering thoughts. Our deep-seated bad habits, having become even more entrenched over thousands of lifetimes, make liberating ourselves solely by our own efforts almost impossible. He knew that to end one's problems and attain lasting happiness many people would need the help of another Buddha: Amitabha, the Buddha of Infinite Light and Infinite Life.

Almost all of the teachings by Sakyamuni were the result of his being asked a question. In a departure from the norm, and when the time was right, Sakyamuni initiated the teaching that introduced Amitabha and his Pure Land. This spontaneous teaching by Sakyamuni is one of the reasons this teaching is so special.

In this teaching, Sakyamuni recounted how the bodhisattva Dharmakara, after witnessing the suffering of sentient beings, spent five eons studying all the Buddha lands. Dharmakara then made forty-eight vows, the fulfillment of which would create the Western Pure Land of Ultimate Bliss. He declared that he would not attain Buddhahood unless his vows for a perfect Pure Land, where all beings would advance along the Buddhist path and never again fall back into samsara, were accomplished. Once his vows were accomplished, Dharmakara Bodhisattva became Amitabha Buddha. He is now speaking the

Dharma in his Pure Land and helping all who are truly sincere in their personal vows to be reborn there.

With help from Amitabha, we do not have to rely solely on ourselves to attain enlightenment as we would with other methods. In Pure Land Buddhism, we rely on the Buddhas and bodhisattvas to help us. Thus, reliance on self and on another are combined as we request by way of our mindful chanting that Amitabha Buddha, through the strength of his vows, help us to be reborn in the Pure Land as we breathe our last breath in our present body.

Amitabha also vowed that once we attain this rebirth, we will always progress in our practice and learning. We will be able to continue our practice in the Pure Land or, when we choose to, return to this and other worlds to help others. We do so without being affected by unfavorable environments or our former bad habits. If we wish, we will be able to do this even before we attain supreme enlightenment.

Amitabha Buddha's Pure Land has innumerable wonders and advantages, all of which arise from the great vows, deeds, and purity of all the beings there. Through his vows, Amitabha helps all beings create the causes to plant the roots of goodness. With his deeds, he creates the conditions for beings to accumulate merits. With his purity, he has created a perfect land, one that is free from pollution, anger, and intolerance. It is a land of peace and serenity. It is a world of equality, joy, and beauty. In comparison, our world is one of delusion and suffering, filled with worry and anxiety.

For countless people, Pure Land practice is the most suitable for several reasons. First, it is relatively easy to practice in almost any environment: alone, with other practitioners, or even amid the hustle and bustle of everyday life.

Second, there are no difficult entry criteria. Even if one's abilities and knowledge are modest, with belief, vows, and practice, we will be reborn in the Pure Land. Belief means that we need to believe in the Buddhas and their teachings, and in causality. We need to believe in ourselves and that we have the same true nature as the Buddha. We need to believe that by living a moral life and being mindful of Amitabha Buddha, we will be born into the Western Pure Land and become a Buddha in one lifetime.

And third, due to the vows of Amitabha, achievement through this method can be attained more quickly and more easily than with other practices. We can understand this better through an analogy. We come to a river that we wish to cross. We can swim across but our baggage is very heavy and the water is treacherously deep. Alternatively, we can get on a boat that will quickly and safely take us and our baggage to the other shore. Symbolically, the "other shore" is the achievement of enlightenment. The baggage we carry is our deep-seated bad habits and negative karmas accumulated over uncountable lifetimes, and the boat is Amitabha Buddha's compassionate will. The ticket to board the boat is belief, the sincere vow to be reborn in the Pure Land, and practice, which includes leading a moral life and mindfully chanting "Amituofo."

The simplest way to practice Pure Land is by chanting "Amituofo." Amituofo is the name of Amitabha Buddha in Chinese. It does not matter whether we chant in Chinese or in any other language as long as we do it properly. When we chant, the sound of "Amituofo" arises in our minds. And as we utter "Amituofo," our minds concentrate on and embrace that sound. While chanting, do so sincerely and continuously.

As one keeps chanting and the mind focuses on the sound of "Amituofo," errant thoughts are replaced with pure thoughts. In this way, we also create less negative karma. After Amitabha has been in our mind continuously for a long time, our true nature—our Buddha-nature—will gradually be uncovered.

Amitabha Buddha is the wise and compassionate teacher who understands everything, and who is always thinking of us, lifetime after lifetime after lifetime.

We are the students who are trying to learn and practice. Just as a good teacher listens to the calls for help from a student looking for the right answers, if we have unwavering belief, vow to be reborn in the Pure Land, and behave morally and sincerely practice, Amitabha will respond. He is like the mother who always thinks of her child. If the child does not in turn think of his mother, her thoughts will not help. But if he also thinks of her, they will eventually be reunited. In such a way, Amitabha is always thinking of us, waiting for our thoughts to turn to him, so that we may come together.

When we chant to the point of single-mindedness with the sole thought of Amituofo, we successfully form a connection with him—in fact, we become one with him. In that instant we are in the Pure Land—far to the west and deep within us. As we breathe our last breath in this world, if we can form this connection—this oneness with Amituofo—we will attain our next rebirth in the Western Pure Land and leave suffering behind. And once there, we will have all the time we need to continue our practice and learning, for we will be in the company of Amitabha Buddha and all the bodhisattvas. They will help us learn all the ways to wisely and compassionately help other beings.

This is why I have chosen the Pure Land path. For me it is the most suitable. It feels absolutely right.

The old monk in the story at the beginning of this book summarized the teaching of the Buddha as "Avoid all that is evil, embrace all that is good, and purify our mind." How? Find a new way. Awaken to a new approach. At every moment of our lives we have a choice. Everything we do will impact others. Everything will eventually come back to us.

We can continue to act based on our erratic thoughts and be pulled frantically one way and then another. Or, we can calm our mind and broaden our heart with compassion, discipline, concentration, and wisdom. We can discover the innate goodness that is already within each one of us.

We can awaken to the Buddha within.

Ways to Reach Us
Internet
www.abrc.org.au
www.amtbweb.org

Australia [61]
Amitabha Buddhist Association of NSW
T: 2-9643-7588   F: 2-9643-7599

Amitabha Buddhist Association of Perth
T: 8-9306-8120   F: 8-9306-8366

Amitabha Buddhist Association of QLD
T: 7-3273-1693   F: 7-3272-0677   E: amtb@amtb-qld.org.au

Amitabha Buddhist Retreat Centre
T: 7-4171-0421   F: 7-4171-0413   E: info@abrc.org.au
www.abrc.org.au

Pure Land Learning Center of the NT
T: 8-8927-4988   F: 8-8981-3516   E: leonel.tchia@palantir.com.au

Pure Land Learning Center of Victoria
T: 3-9891-7093   F: 9891-7093   E: purelandvic@yahoo.com

Pure Land Learning College (Toowoomba)
T: 7-4637-8765   F: 7-4637-8764   E: purelandcollege@iinet.net.au
www.chinkung.org   www.amtb-aus.org

Canada [1]
Ottawa Amitabha Buddhist Association of Canada
T: 613-723-9683   F: 613-723-6316   E: info@amtb-ottawa.ca
www.amtb-ottawa.ca

Amitabha (Six Harmony) Buddhist Organization
T: 416-265-9838   F: 905-947-1870   E: amtb6hcan@yahoo.ca

Amitabha Buddhist Society of Montreal
T: 514-257-1770   F: 514-525-6846   E: amtbmtl@hotpop.com

Amitabha Buddhist Society of Toronto
T: 416-293-0024   F: 416-292-6061

Infinite Light Amitabha Organization of Canada
Tel: 416-893-3366/265-9838 Fax: 905-947-1870 E: infamtb@yahoo.cz

United Kingdom [44]
Buddhist Education Foundation (UK)
T: 171-586-6923   F: 171-794-8594   E: info@buddhisteducation.co.uk
www.buddhisteducation.co.uk

Hong Kong [852]
Hong Kong Buddhist Education Foundation
T: 2314-7099   F: 2314-1929   E: amtbhk1@budaedu.org.hk

Malaysia [60]
Amitabha Buddhist Society (Malaysia)
T: 03-4041-4101   F: 03-4041-2172   E: amtbmy@amtb-m.org.my
www.amtb-m.org.my/emid.shtml

Singapore [65]
Amitabha Buddhist Society (S)
T: 6744-7444   F: 6744-4774   E: abss@amtb.org.sg

Singapore Buddhist Lodge
T: 6737-2630   F: 6737-0877   E: sbl@sbl.org.sg

Taiwan [886]
The Corporation Republic of Hwa Dzan Society
T: 02-2754.7178   F: 02-2754-7262
www.amtb.org.tw

Thailand (662)
Amitabha Buddhist Society
T: 662-719-5206   F: 662-719-4356

United States of America [1]
Amida Society
T: 626-286-5700   F: 626-286-7988   E: amtbla@pacbell.net

Amita Buddhism Society-Boston
T/F: 508-580-4349   E: amtb_boston@yahoo.com

Amitabha Buddhist Association of State Washington
T: 425-251-6822   F: 425-656-9789

Amitabha Buddhist Library in Chicago
T: 630-416-9422   F: 630-416-6175   E: info@amitabhalibrary.org
www.amitabhalibrary.org

Amitabha Buddhist Society of Hawaii
T/F: 808-523-8909

Amitabha Buddhist Society of Houston
T: 713-339-1864   F: 713-339-2242

Amitabha Buddhist Society of Michigan
T: 734-995-5132   F: 734-995-5132

Amitabha Buddhist Society of New Jersey, Inc.
T: 856-751-7966   F: 856-751-2269   E: njbuddha@comcast.net

Amitabha Buddhist Society of NY, Inc.
T: 718-961-7299 F: 718-961-8039   E: amitabha_ny@yahoo.com.tw

Amitabha Buddhist Society of Philadelphia
T: 856-424-2516   F: 856-489-8528   E: amtbphila@hotmail.com

Amitabha Buddhist Society of Seattle
T: 206-624-9378

Amitabha Buddhist Society at UK
www.ku.edu/~amtb

Amitabha Buddhist Society of USA
T: 408-736-3386   F: 408-736-3389   E: info@amtb-usa.org
www.amtb-usa.org

Amitabha Educational Center (Hawaii)
T: 808-262-5279   F: 808-262-498

Amitabha Society of Las Vegas
T: 707-252-3042   F: 707-871-3542

Atlanta Amitabha Buddhist Society
T: 770-923-8955   F: 770-925-0618   E: mietoville@bellsouth.net

Dallas Buddhist Association
T: 972-234-4401   F: 972-234-8342   E: amtbdba@yahoo.com
www.amtb-dba.org